The California Deserts

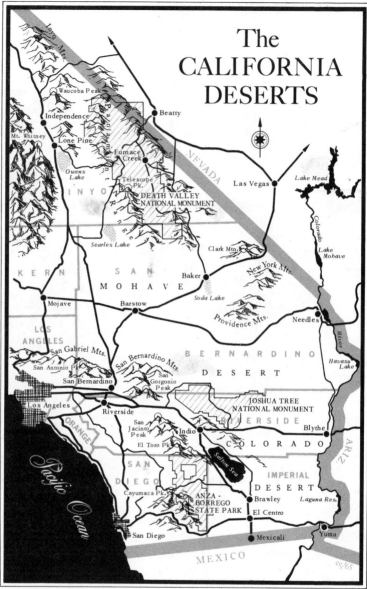

The
CALIFORNIA
DESERTS

The California Deserts

Edmund C. Jaeger

Fourth Edition

Stanford University Press, Stanford, California

By the same author

The North American Deserts
Desert Wildlife
Desert Wild Flowers

Stanford University Press
Stanford, California
Copyright 1933 and 1938 by the Board of Trustees of the Leland
Stanford Junior University. Copyright renewed 1961 and 1965 by
Edmund C. Jaeger. Copyright © 1955 and 1965 by the Board of
Trustees of the Leland Stanford Junior University.
Printed in the United States of America
ISBN 0-8047-1223-9
Original edition 1933
Fourth edition, 1965
Last figure below indicates year of this printing:
92 91 90 89 88 87 86 85 84 83

Preface

In the more than thirty years since the publication of the first edition of my *California Deserts* many major changes have taken place in the desert area as a result of the influx of settlers, the expansion of agriculture, the building of modern roads and towns, and the use of some of the deserts' most wild and attractive parts by the Army and Navy for testing modern weapons of warfare. But although much has been taken from us there yet remains much to see and appreciate. There are still wide expanses of wilderness area to explore and camp in. It is surprising how short is the distance off the main traveled roads to places where primitive desert conditions yet prevail. Fortunately there are to this day many places where one may dwell for weeks at a time while enjoying perfect solitude and see nature still unspoiled by the encroachments of man.

To help the seeker after desert knowledge appreciate more fully many of the scenic wonders of the deserts' solitary places, a goodly number of excellent photographic illustrations were added. The name of the camera artist is given below each picture. The flower illustrations are all my own work and were made from living plants. W. A. Sharp made the delightful ink drawings which head the chapters and add atmosphere to the pages. Miss Pauline Hearst made line drawings of the animals. The bibliography has been brought up to date, and many major changes have been made in the text.

I am under great and continuing obligation to the following persons for their many aids and suggestions: Rodolfo Riubal, Lloyd Mason Smith, Ivan Brady, John F. Goins, Richard H. Tedford, Vincent D. Roth, Lon McClanahan, Oscar Clarke, William Hodson, and Lauren D. Anderson.

EDMUND C. JAEGER

Riverside, California
September 15, 1965

Contents

1. Introduction   1

2. The Desert's Past   5

3. Physiographic Aspects   17

4. Weather and Climatic Features   34

5. Insects and Other Invertebrates   42

6. Fishes, Frogs, and Toads   66

7. Reptile Life   71

8. Birds   84

9. Mammalian Life   99

10. The Aborigines of the Desert   112

11. Botanical Aspects of Arid Regions   122

12. Fungi, Ferns, and Grasses   150

13. Shrubs   158

14. Trees   174

15. Travel Hints   184

16. The Preservation of Deserts   189

Selected References   195

Index   203

Illustrations

Washingtonia Palms, Salton Basin	1
Erosional Forms, Red Rock Canyon, Mohave Desert	5
Maps of Pleistocene and Present Lake Areas of the Great Basin	6
Map of Lakes and Rivers of the Ancient Mohave Region	7
Cinder Cone, Mohave Desert	17
Goblet Valleys, Panamint Trough	19
Section Through a Cinder Cone and Lava Flow	20
Cima Dome, Mohave Desert	23
Rock Plain and Mountain	24
Clouded Skies and Flower Fields, Colorado Desert	34
Devil's Garden, Salton Basin	42
Some Desert Insects	52
Curious Insect Homes	58
Box Canyon, Colorado Desert	66
Sand Ripples on Dunes, Mohave Desert	71
Some Desert Lizards	72
More Desert Lizards	75
Heads of Some Desert Snakes	82
Tree Yuccas (Joshua Trees), Mohave Desert	84
Some Desert Birds	88
More Desert Birds	90
Barrel Cacti and Clay Hills, Colorado Desert	99
Some Desert Mammals	100
Indian Petroglyphs	112
Flower Fields in Spring	122
Wild Flower Illustrations	127–49
Grasses in a Desert Basin	150
Desert Fungi	151
Some Desert Ferns	155
Deerhorn Cactus and Smaller Shrubs	158
Some Desert Cacti	169

More Desert Cacti 171

Palo Verde Tree in Box Canyon, Colorado Desert 174

Some Desert Trees, Details 175

More Desert Trees, Details 177

Indian Trail and Ceremonial Piles 184

Alluvial Fan and Rocky Hills, Mohave Desert 189

Photographic Section

The following are illustrated in the photographic section, between pages 50 and 51: Saltbushes along the Amargosa River. Palo verde; mountains of red volcanic rocks. Limestone caverns; desert willows. *Yucca brevifolia Jaegeriana*; Mohave yucca; Weber Joshua tree. Erosional forms. Eroded granites. Crescentic dunes; the Pinnacles. Sand dunes; desert tortoise. Stand of creosote bush. Desert dry-lake; house finch nestlings. Spade-foot toad; antelope ground squirrel; bobcat; ant crater. Designs in sand; barrel cactus. Deerhorn cactus; *Pilostyles thurberi*. Desert fan palm; sand verbena. Desert bighorn. Smoke tree.

The California Deserts

*We can enjoy things more, the more
we know about them. Simply to be
able to call the elements of beauty by
their right names helps us to relive
them. Intellectually to grasp an object
of enjoyment is to possess it more
securely. We take more pleasure in
the stars if we know their names.
We listen better to birds if we can
distinguish them. We hear a symphony
with deeper absorption if we know
something of its harmonies.*

—Walter Russell Bowie

1. Introduction

Lord Bryce has said that "renunciation is the hardest part of travel," and I would add that discovery is its greatest joy. And so, while I have made this a guidebook for the desert traveler, I have tried not to make everything so obvious as to remove the enchantment of novelty or the joy of seeking for hidden treasure. I have told about many of the things there are to discover, but have left it for the reader to detect where the nuggets lie ensconced.

The geographical, geological, and other natural history features of our desert domains are so varied and with them are bound up so many entrancing problems that fifty years of intimate acquaintance and wide travel over the arid Southwest have not desiccated my ardor for continued study and wide wanderings nor lessened my eagerness to lead others to the heart of my kingdom of joy.

The question "What is a desert?" cannot be answered without facing many difficulties. The term desert does not necessarily imply paucity of life, continuous heat, marked lack of moisture, or the presence of sandy wastes, although all these phenomena may occur. Even meagerness of rainfall is not always the deciding factor in the making of deserts but is only one of a combination of factors. Rocky or alkaline soils and continuous winds are features which play no minor role.

For our present purposes, deserts may be defined as places of high, diurnal, summer temperatures, with more or less steady, drying winds and slight rainfall (generally under ten inches a year) and that unevenly and, from the standpoint of all but specialized plants and animals, often very unsatisfactorily distributed.

A little map study will reveal the fact that a surprisingly large portion of the globe is desert or semidesert. Deserts have avoided the equatorial area and have chosen to lie "a little to the north of the northern tropic and a little to the south of the southern tropic" (Buxton). They constitute two broad belts lying for the most part directly under the trade winds and extending well across the continents. It is these trade winds that furnish the most important cause of deserts. Of great regularity and always athirst, they sweep over the lands and rob them of their moisture. The deserts of Southwestern United States lie north of the belt of trades but are visited by offshore winds of the upper atmosphere, which are almost equally powerful causes of aridity. In December the south and southwesterly winds begin to bring rains to the Pacific Coast, but their moisture is largely dissipated by the lofty mountains before they reach the desert.

The largest of all deserts, the great Palearctic, stretches with certain minor interruptions from the Atlantic shores of northern Africa to northwestern India and far into the center of China. It includes the great Sahara, the deserts of Arabia, Iran, Turkan, Thar, Kara Kum, Kizil Kum, Takla Makan, and the Gobi. The second largest arid area comprises the enormous interior plains of Australia, sometimes spoken of as the dead heart of the continent. Next in extent are the North American deserts, occupying much of the Great Basin; reaching west and south they extend almost to the California coast and into Mexico.

Minor but specialized deserts exist in southwestern Africa,

in eastern Patagonia, in western Argentina, in the provinces of Atacama and Antofagasta in Chile, and in southern Peru. Each desert is to some extent the counterpart of every other; they have much in common. Each is an interior basin of irregular relief, surrounded, at least in part, by mountain masses or high plateaus which serve as barriers robbing the incoming winds of their moisture. In the midst of each of them are inland seas or lakes, and several have areas which dip below the level of the sea. The Caspian, the Dead Sea, and the Sea of Aral lie in the deserts of Asia, Great Salt Lake and the Salton Sea in arid North America, and Lake Eyre in the interior of Australia.

The area here treated embraces both the Mohave (Mo-hah'-vay) and the Colorado Desert of southeastern California and also certain contiguous portions of southern Nevada and western Arizona, all within the realm of the creosote bush, that remarkable plant which marks better than any other the domain of the real Sonoran desert.

The Colorado Desert includes not only the area immediately contiguous to the Colorado River but also the Salton Basin and the rather low-lying bordering areas which drain into the Salton Sink. This agrees well with the conception of W. P. Blake, who first gave the Colorado Desert its name in 1853. From the biological standpoint the northern limit of the Colorado Desert may be arbitrarily placed as far north as a line drawn from the Morongo Pass easterly to the Colorado River. The Mohave is a high, somewhat quadrangular-shaped desert with an altitude varying from 2,000 to well over 5,000 feet. Except for a small area along the Colorado River, none of the waters which fall upon it reach the ocean, but sink into the desert sands to be evaporated by the unremitting, dry, and often hot winds. Its western and southern boundaries are the San Gabriel and San Bernardino mountains. To the north and east it stretches up into the Death Valley area and across the broad basins of eastern California into southeastern

Nevada. The transition from one desert to the other is gradual but nonetheless definite, as is shown by the changing flora and fauna. To understand the differences these deserts show in physiography, climate, and plant and animal life, we must inquire as fully as possible into the peculiar history of their past.

2. The Desert's Past

The desert's geologic history is one long series of changes. Deposits of limestones, sandstones, and other fossil-bearing rocks scattered widely but particularly evident in the far eastern and northern Mohave Desert indicate that in ancient geological times (Cambrian and Carboniferous) much of the region was at least twice covered by the sea.

After these ancient periods of sea submergence the land was upraised, forming a high upland area of bold relief. But the erosive agencies of wind and water, both during the upheaval and afterward, were busy and during the long succeeding ages wore the country down until only broad lowlands diversified by hills and mere ridges were left. During periods designated by the geologists as early and middle Tertiary, volcanoes burst forth and repeatedly covered the land far and wide with deep accumulations of lava, mud, and ash, the remains of which are still widely seen. Volcanic outbreaks continued intermittently and with decreasing vigor until Pliocene and late Quaternary times.

Even more important than the Tertiary period of vulcanism was the alteration of the older topography by the slow upthrusting of the Sierra Nevada, the San Gabriel, the San Bernardino, and the San Jacinto mountains, as well as the

numerous ranges of the Great Basin area. The upheaval of
these enormous blocks of the earth's crust was not a single
cataclysmic event, sudden and violent, but a series of successive uplifts beginning in the late Tertiary and extending almost up to our times. The causes which initiated these crustal
movements are not fully known, but the significance of the
event is great, for as an inevitable consequence there came
marked alterations of the climate and changes in the adjacent
drainage systems. Many of the streams which formerly passed
to the oceans were dislocated and forced to carry their sediments into undrained interior basins.

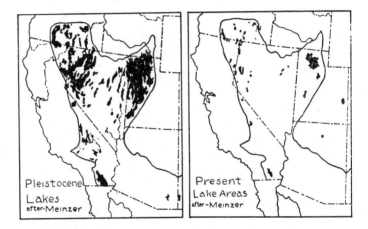

When first we visit the desert and see the present broad,
flat-floored, sun-drenched basins,* the verdureless, sharp-
crested mountains, and the dry streamways, it seems unnat-
ural to picture it as once having had a more humid climate
and many large lakes. Yet all the evidence produced by the
geologists points to the fact that such a land it was in times

* The term basin (not valley) is the appropriate one to use when speaking
of the undrained mountain- or hill-rimmed depressions of the desert
area. A valley is a *drained* troughlike depression with inbranching tribu-
taries cut under the leadership of running water.

(Pleistocene) which succeeded the period of mountain building just mentioned. The accompanying maps, contrasting the
present lake areas of the Great Basin with their abundance
during recent geologic ages, show in unmistakable manner
the climatic changes which have since taken place. In many
places where now are dry gravel slopes or *bajadas* and arid,
deep-set basins, running streams and bodies of living water
then offered sanctuary to wild fowl, wading birds, and other
small creatures. In regions now so barren that only a few wild
mice can gain sustenance from the seeds borne by small,
scrubby plants, large mammals such as the mastodon, camel,
and ancient horse found a sufficiency of green food.

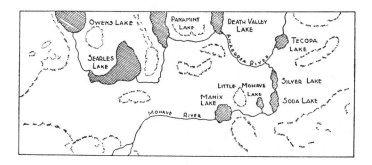

Lake Bonneville, fed to its fullness by streams derived from
the more plentiful rains and the melting glaciers of the lofty
Wasatch Range and other high ranges, once covered almost
one-third of the area of the present state of Utah. The basin
of the former Lake Lahontan (La-hon'-tan), occupying a series of confluent depressions, principally in the western half
of Nevada, was filled by the mighty streams from the snow
and glaciers of the Sierra Nevada.

That there were many climatic oscillations in this time of
recent lake formation, that is, periods of drought interspersed
between long cycles of wet seasons, cannot be doubted by
those who see, about the margins of the old lake basins, the

well-marked and beautifully preserved beach terraces and other shore features which indicate the different levels reached and maintained over considerable periods by the waters. The high-water stages indicated by the highest shore lines probably correspond to the different glacial epochs. In the Lahontan Basin there are records of three and perhaps four distinct lake stages. During the interglacial epochs, the basins were deserts much as they are today.

If we turn to the recent lacustrine history of the Mohave and Colorado deserts we have a most fascinating story with its scenes laid at our very doors. The author can suggest no more instructive and inspiring journey than a trip tracing the course of some of the ancient drainage channels and the sites of the placid lakes that once occupied our near desert basins.

To the east of the bold Sierra which form the rocky backbone of California are four large, longitudinal, almost furrowlike depressions separated by parallel ranges of desolate, steep-pitched mountains. In each of these troughs there were basins which became at this time of more humid climate the sites of ancient lakes. Streams derived from rains and melting Sierran glaciers provided the waters which formed these lakes and linked them into a quite peculiar and well-defined series.

The first of the lakes to appear occupied a flat at the lower end of Owens Valley. It was a deep body of fresh water very much larger than the present shrunken salina, the white, almost dry, salt-encrusted surface of which we now see glistening like a blanket of snow on the desert floor. The strands and gravel bars, marking by their levels the varying depths of its waters and the climatic fluctuations of those distant times, are plainly visible even to this day as we travel along the motor highway skirting the western shores of Owens Lake. The fact that they appear so fresh is convincing evidence that the lake cannot be so very old when compared to the much-worn mountains which rise in steep pitches to the east and west of it. Overflowing its southern brink during periods of high water, the lake sent a stream into the broad, shallow basin known as Indian Wells Valley, thence onward through Salt Wells Valley to Searles Basin. Here another large lake was formed which at its highest stage not only covered most of the Searles Basin but backed up through Salt Wells Valley westward into Indian Wells Valley. A good idea of its size may be gained by observing on the sides of the encircling mountains the abandoned shore lines. These stand out with remarkable clearness on the bold and rugged Slate Range when viewed from the south side of the lake just after sunrise. The highest of them shows that this body of water once stood more than 600 feet above the floor of the present basin. A remarkable group of steep crags made of calcareous tufa precipitated from the waters with the aid of algae or bacteria are found at the southwest end of Searles Lake. These spectacular rocks, often called the Pinnacles, rise about 100 feet above the parched desert plain and remind one of the tall conical termite nests found in tropical Africa. They are scattered singly or in clusters over an area of several square miles, forming a major scenic attraction.

When Searles Lake was at its highest level, its excess waters spilled from its southern end over into a low trough known as Pilot Knob Valley, and after pursuing an eastward course turned north and filled a basin in the deep Panamint Trough. Here another great body of water over 900 feet deep and fully 60 miles long reflected from its mirrored surface the light from a more temperate sun. Brimming to its full capacity, Panamint Lake probably discharged through Wingate Pass into Death Valley, where the fourth and fifth of this chain of prehistoric lakes, Lake Manly and the contemporary smaller Lake Rogers, were established.

With the drying of the climate, all the lakes acted as concentration basins for the salts that had been leached out from the rocks and carried into them by inflowing streams. In the lowest parts of the basins, the saline deposits, mixed with alluvium carried down from the surrounding hills, formed con-

spicuous playas or mud flats. Some of them are surfaced with
a smooth, hard floor of clay; others, however, are covered with
rough, buffy-brown layers of dried mud. After heavy seasonal
rains or after cloudbursts the expansive flats are sometimes
covered with water, but to a depth of only a few inches.

In Searles Lake is a deep-lying deposit of unusually pure
salts, from 60 to 100 feet thick, known as the crystal body. It
is from this mineral storehouse that the American Potash and
Chemical Company pumps the brines from which it recovers
so many commercially valuable products. No such rich deposits have been found in Death Valley or Panamint Lake,
but Owens Lake has yielded large amounts of valuable salts.
They are found concentrated in the form of carbonates,
sulphates, chlorides, and borates.

Just as the Owens River acted as the feeder for a series of
lakes, so the Mohave River formed during this same humid
period a chain of lakes along its course. The uplifting of the
San Bernardino and San Gabriel mountains in late Tertiary
times provoked increased rainfall and greatly augmented previous drainage. It presumably better developed this stream
which we now call the Mohave River. It must then have been
a river of considerable size, for even in the arid climate of
today it flows above ground or beneath the surface of the
sands for 145 miles across the desert wastes. Freighted with
gravels, sands, and clays, the reinforced river built up an
enormous outwash plain, which stretched to the northward
as far as the hills near the present site of Victorville. After
wandering for a time back and forth over the surface of its
flood plain, it finally established for itself a permanent course.
But in wearing down its channel it met some hard rock masses
(really tops of granite hills) which lay buried beneath the
river bed; and, following the habit of rivers in such cases, it
cut a channel through them. The small but impressive gorge
which was eroded constitutes the First Narrows of the Mohave just to the south of Victorville. The tracks of the Santa

Fe Railway now lie in the ancient cut. A little farther to the north the stream wore down a channel through a second group of similar rocks. A river acting as this one did is called by the geologists a superimposed river because the present stream channel was superimposed on the old granite hills. Both above and below the Narrows the river cut a channel in a broad flood plain of alluvium.

About 40 miles east of Barstow it entered a depression rimmed on the east by the much folded, faulted, and eroded Cave Mountain and Cady Mountain. The basin caused the river to expand into a shallow lake, which eventually covered an area of at least 200, perhaps 300, square miles. The geologists refer to it as Lake Manix because a railroad station of that name lies in the midst of the old beds. Following a dry period when the area was converted into a playa, and a time of deposition of alluvial sediments, the lake reappeared. The accumulating waters at last found a point of egress at the basin's northeast end, and a channel was cut which finally became so deep that the lake was completely drained. The large gorge through which the stream poured is known as Cave Canyon. Passengers on the Union Pacific Railroad may view its picturesquely eroded and highly colored walls as the train passes between Afton and Baxter, about 42 miles east of Barstow. It is one of the great scenic attractions of the Mohave region. The Spanish priest Fray Francisco Garcés in 1776 passed through this canyon on his way from the Mohave Indian villages on the Colorado River to the Mission San Gabriel. To the "arroyo of saltish waters" he gave the name Arroyo de los Martires.*

* The Mohave River Valley was the great roadway along which the early travelers passed into and out of southern California. The reasons are obvious: it furnished water for the human travelers and both food and water for their animals. Hither passed the American trapper, Jedediah Smith, also Kit Carson, Frémont, and Dr. Lyman. It was Frémont who gave the river its name. From him we have that old spelling, "Mohahve." The Old Spanish Trail followed eastward along the Mohave River as far

The greenish alluvium of the old Lake Manix beds may be observed at the head of Cave Gorge. In the canyon proper it is overlain by spectacular, red-buff conglomerates. Dr. Buwalda of the California Institute of Technology found in these Lake Manix clays fossil remains of a mastodon, an antelope, camels, horses, and a bird, all considered to be of Pleistocene age.

Emerging at the lower end of Cave Canyon, the Mohave River entered the upper reaches of a great north-south intermont trough which stretches with but minor interruptions to the lower end of Death Valley. It now began wandering in crooked ways over its outwash plain of detritus. The grade was so slight that at times the stream passed along a northward radius of its fan into Cronese Basin and established a shallow lake of sufficient permanence to encourage the growth of mollusks. The usual course of the river was then, as it is at present, eastward, and it finally entered Soda Lake, an enormous playa appropriately called the Sink of the Mohave. The volume of water which at times came down from the mountains must have been considerable, for, after filling Soda Lake Basin, now and then the river overflowed northward across an inbuilt dividing fan to Silver Lake Basin and at last to Death Valley, which, as indicated above, is but a natural extension of the trough. The Los Angeles–Salt Lake highway crosses Soda Lake at Baker Station, and the Death Valley road passes along the entire length of Silver Lake.

---

as Soda Lake, where it turned northward along Silver Lake and Silurian Dry Lake to a spring of bitter waters called Salt Spring. Sometimes travelers broke away from the river route at a point a little to the east of the Calico Mountains and continued by way of Bitter Springs and along the east side of the Avawatz Range to Salt Springs. From this point of meeting, all travelers passed northward along the sandy wash of the Amargosa River until near the present site of Tecopa, where they turned eastward through Resting Springs and Stump Springs, climbed a pass in the south end of the scenic Spring Mountain Range, and then made their way to Vegas Spring.

Death Valley received the final flow of still another ancient river, the Amargosa, or river of bitter waters, which arose then, as it does today, in one of the sequestered intermont troughs to the east of Death Valley. Though its catchment area was larger than that of the Mohave River and one of the most extensive in the Great Basin, the stream probably never discharged a large quantity of water into the Death Valley Lake (Lake Manly). Death Valley Lake was so short-lived that presumably no well-cut terraces were ever formed about its rim.

In geologic times the Amargosa and the Mohave rivers united before they reached Death Valley. At the present time the salty Amargosa occasionally reaches Death Valley when heavy winter rains or cloudbursts augment the usual meager flow; but the Mohave River, even during the wettest seasons, never gets farther than Silver Lake and generally no farther than Soda Lake.

"Probably at some time at the end of the Tertiary period," says L. F. Noble, "the waters of the Amargosa River were ponded in Amargosa Valley and a lake was formed in which beds of clay, sand, and gravel were deposited. These deposits cover all the floor of the valley between Tecopa and a point north of Shoshone and extend several hundred feet up the slopes on the sides of the valley—their total thickness probably does not exceed 400 feet. These beds cover an area of at least 100 square miles, which indicates approximately the maximum extent of the lake. After the basin of the lake was filled with sediments, possibly to the level of its outlet, the Amargosa River began to cut down through the barrier to lower its bed. Since that time it has carved for itself, below Tecopa, a deep, rocky canyon which is one of the striking scenic features of the region. As the river bed was progressively deepened, the base-level of the Amargosa Valley above the barrier was lowered; and the lake deposits were subjected to erosion. As a result they have been dissected almost to their base, so that over most of the area in which they are exposed they now form mesas and badlands."

This remarkable region of badland topography is all too often overlooked by the traveler as he passes northward toward Shoshone on the Silver Lake–Death Valley road.

At the head of the Gulf of California lies the Salton or Cahuilla Basin, a narrow depression, nearly 100 miles long, set between the Peninsular Range on the southwest and the Little San Bernardino and Chocolate mountains on the northeast. It forms the larger part of what we generally call the Colorado Desert, a name given because of its close proximity to the lower end of the Colorado River. Like the Mohave Desert, which borders it on the north and east, its most interesting recent geological history is bound up with lake formation and a river which ran into it.

The Salton Sink, wherein now lies the Salton Sea, is a depression some 273 feet below sea level. It is thought to have been formed by the slow sinking of a 200-mile-long block of the earth's crust at the same time that surrounding mountain ranges on either side were being elevated. This fault-depressed region or "graben" would now be nearly filled with water from the sea, at least as far north as Indio, if it were not for the natural fanlike deltaic dam which the Colorado River built across its lower end, where for ages it discharged its tremendous loads of silt into the upper end of the Gulf of California. During heavy floods, its course across the low-lying delta changed and it overflowed, sometimes northward into the Salton Sink or westward into another shallower sink now occupied by the Laguna Salada.

In more recent times, but still many, many hundreds of years ago, the Rio Colorado discharged into the Sink for a long period and formed a fresh-water sea over 100 miles long and 35 miles across at its widest point. To this ancient body of water the geologists have given the name Lake Le Conte in memory of J. N. Le Conte, who made early studies of the Sink. Especially along the spurs of the Santa Rosa Mountains are the well-defined beach lines and wave-cut terraces of this prehistoric lake evident.

This first of two ancient Lake Le Contes was probably an interglacial or postglacial fresh-water body obviously younger than the Pluvial Lake chains of the Great Basin and Mohave Desert regions. It may have been in existence several thousand years. A shifting of the course of the Colorado River was followed by a long dry period. It is thought that there was a second high filling of Lake Le Conte in rather recent times. It had a duration from about A.D. 1000 to A.D. 1450 or 1500. Recent fossil evidence seems to indicate that the lower areas of the present Salton Sink were covered at least twice by the sea. The first sea invasion was before the Salton Basin existed. The last covering by the sea may have taken place between the two fresh-water stages. After the water of the last high Lake Le Conte evaporated there was left but a salt-encrusted playa with only a small salt marsh in its center, kept moist by few springs and occasional cloudbursts and winter rain freshets. And so it remained until very recent times.

The present Salton Sea is about 47 miles in length and about 17 miles in width at its widest point. It was formed in 1905–7 when a break in the irrigation system of the Imperial Valley, caused by summer floods of the Gila and Colorado rivers, allowed enormous quantities of river water to enter the Salton Basin. The sea formed by the two-year inflow described by W. P. Blake had "a length of 45 miles, a maximum breadth of 17 miles, and a total area of 410 square miles, with a maximum depth of 83 feet." In 1907 water entering the Salton Sea was controlled by dumping brush mats and enormous quantities of rock brought in by the Southern Pacific Company. The whole effort cost over $2,000,000.

Upon completion of Hoover Dam in the late 1930's, more water for irrigation of the tillable lands of the Salton Basin was made available and more water was allowed to "waste" into the sea. In 1956 the water level of the sea was −234.5 feet. The surface elevation in 1907 was −195 feet. By 1925 it had fallen to −250 feet. The maximum depth in 1956 was about 40 feet. In 1956 the salinity of the water was only a little less than the total contents of ocean water.

3. Physiographic Aspects

Our desert scenery is probably affected more by the presence
of mountains than by any other geological feature. The mo-
notony of the pale-faced basins is everywhere broken by the
stern but colorful peaks and massive ridges which protrude
islandlike from the vast seas of sand and gravel. Some of the
mountains rise abruptly from the desert floor; others ascend
by long, smooth, concave slopes. Many, according to Wm. M.
Davis, "have suffered so large a measure of erosion that their
well-developed slopes have been worn back a mile or more,
leaving an even rock floor or 'pediment,' veneered with thin
patches of subangular gravel slanting gently forward to an
intermont detrital plain." The bare rocky flanks are slashed
by innumerable intricately embranched gullies or shallow
but often tortuous valleys. Extending from the mouths of the
boulder-strewn canyons are broad outwash fans consisting of
a mixture of rocks, coarse gravels, sand, and silt which have
been flushed from the mountain valleys. Coalescing, these
outwash fans form broad alluvial aprons, which gradually
slope downward in beautiful sweeping curves to the centers
of the basins. From a scenic standpoint I know of few features
more appealing than these long, sloping fans when seen in
profile. In the case of some of the older, much-eroded moun-

tains, the fans reach almost to the crests and the worn-down cores appear to be buried in their own debris.

The powerful forces of deformation to which the earth was subjected in recent geological times produced in the Great Basin area great systems of intersecting or parallel crustal fractures. This desert province was thus broken into huge blocks and splinters, some of which, relatively or actually uplifted, more or less tilted, and carved down, formed our present mountains; intervening blocks sinking or remaining at levels relatively lower formed troughs which since have been deeply filled with detritus from the worn-down mountains. The axes of these fault-block mountain ranges, like the major faults along which they arose, in general extend in a north and south direction. The Sierra Nevada and the ranges of the Death Valley area partake of this same northerly and southerly parallel arrangement, but the majority of the desert mountains to the southwest (i.e., in the mid-Mohave and eastern Colorado deserts), though associated with faulting,* seem to form no coordinated system, their major axes lying in almost every direction.

Among the many earth fissures of the desert area, the Garlock fault, located in the northern Mohave Desert, may be mentioned as an important example of one of our distinctly up-and-down mountain-making faults. This great crustal fracture begins near Tejon Pass, passes along the southeast base of the Paso Mountains, along the southern border of Searles Basin to the lower end of the Slate Range, and then eastward perhaps to the Avawatz Mountains—a total length of 200 miles! Along much of its eastern part it is what we might call an almost obliterated, worn-out fault; but along its middle and western portions motion has been so recent that one easily sees breaks it has caused in the mountain scarps and in several of the alluvial fans it crosses.

* By faulting is meant the displacement of huge rock masses along fractures in the earth's crust.

The Death Valley and the Panamint faults appeal to our interest because of the recent renewal of their activities and because of the enormous escarpments or rock slopes that have been formed along them on the east sides of their respective "valleys." "When they are better known," says L. F. Noble, "they will undoubtedly constitute one of the classic geologic features of Western America." In the Panamint Trough the escarpment, astonishingly fresh at its base, rises in a remarkable, huge, sloping, surface. The accompanying illustration shows the wide valleys which were eroded back into an earlier uplifted scarp. It is evident that the mountains thus carved were again uplifted, carrying the valleys high up on their slopes. The present drainage of these old valleys is through deep, ragged parallel slots cut in the surface of the newly exposed, almost smooth-faced rock slope below them. Small debris cones, recently built at the lower end of the slots, complete the picture of a goblet or wineglass; hence the appropriateness of the term "goblet valleys" that has been applied to them. The Panamint escarpment, seen to great advantage from the pass between Trona and Ballarat, is indeed one of the most impressive spectacles of that very remarkable region.

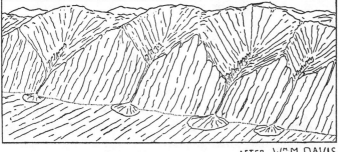

AFTER Wᵐ M. DAVIS

The San Andreas rift is probably the longest earth fissure of the North American continent: it is perhaps even longer than the enormous Rift Valley fault in the east of Africa. It

may be taken as an example of a fault the complicated movements of which, mostly horizontal, are largely unrelated to
mountain building. On the Mohave Desert this great linear
earth fissure lies near the northern base of the San Gabriel
Mountains. Continuing southeastward, after obliquely crossing a shoulder of this range, the master fault cuts the south
base of the San Bernardino Mountains, then passes southeastward near the San Gorgonio Pass and along the northeast
side of the Salton Basin, where it loses itself in the silts bordering the Salton Sea. "The group of mud volcanoes and solfa-
taras at the lower end of the Salton Sea," says Walter C. Mendenhall, "may well be associated with a profound fracture of
this nature."

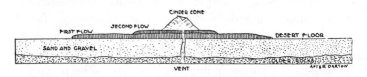

Rivaling the work of mountain-building forces in changing the face of the land have been the forces of vulcanism.
The wide dispersal of lavas and cinder cones in our desert
regions bears testimony to the large-scale activity of volcanoes
in the past. The black lava flows form a scenic feature that is
appealing to every traveler. The unique form of the cinder
cones and their isolation in the broad basins or atop the barren, chocolate-colored ranges is almost startling when seen for
the first time. The materials of which the cones are composed
are the cooled fragments of lava which were thrown out from
the vents, probably at the close of the eruption. The fact that
most of the cones are comparatively low and broad indicates
that the explosions were short-lived but violent, probably
lasting a few hours or at most a few days. Throughout southwestern Utah (what perfect cones there are near Yeyo!),
across southern Nevada, and into eastern and southeastern

California there must be more than a hundred of these cones, each showing some grace of line or other feature of scenic charm.

Excellent views of lava flows and cinder cones of recent origin (Pleistocene and later) may be had at Lavic, at Amboy, in Owens Valley, and in the northern end of Death Valley. A group of twenty-seven cinder cones all huddled together in a small area is visible from the state highway between Baker and Halloran Spring. They lie directly to the south near the Kelso Dunes. The Amboy cone, typical of many others, is well described by Darton. He says: "In the center of the basin, not far southwest of Amboy there is a cinder cone on an extensive sheet of black lava (basalt). This lava is geologically very recent and may have flowed out over the bottom of the basin within the last thousand years. It covers a nearly circular area about five miles in diameter. Its surface is remarkably rough, being covered with large blisters, most of them broken, and it has many caverns where the hot lava has run out at lower levels as it congealed at the surface. All the rock is black, practically unchanged by weathering, and full of vesicles or small holes, due to the escape of steam carried by the molten lava. The edge of the sheet is irregular, just as the lava congealed at the margin of the flow. The cone which is near the center of the flow is about 200 feet high. It consists of a pile of black or dark-gray cinders or pumice, with a large crater at the center. In its southwest side there is a deep breach, from which extends a thin later sheet of lava that flowed over the main sheet."

A short distance beyond Newberry and to the south of Troy station is a cone remarkable because it is mounted high on the mountains. From its borders may be traced the course of the lava stream which flowed from its vent down a narrow valley almost to the level of the highway. As the traveler approaches the narrow-throated entrance to Owens Valley at Little Lake there is to the right a group of similarly high-mounted cones and he may see where the viscid lava on its descent down steep canyons plunged over precipices and congealed in the perfect likeness of waterfalls. One needs little imagination to picture the blowing cones and the glowing red lava as it poured down the gorges in the blackness of a desert night.

From points along the crooked desert road which leads from Fenner north to Cima can be seen a most spectacular formation of deep-red volcanic rocks in which have been eroded an unusual number of large pocketlike recesses, caves, tunnels, shallow alcoves, and deep, slotlike gorges. Beyond are hills capped by erosion-resisting tabular malapais and several picturesque, flat-topped mesas or table mountains, really residual hills on which remain parts of the great lava sheet that once covered much of the desert country. These monuments of erosion are made up of colorful sheets of consolidated volcanic ash, separated by layers of light-colored lavas, and look "just like chocolate layer cakes," as a lad once said to me. The region is well worth a visit.

Black Mountain, northwest of Barstow, cloaked with black basic lavas, marks the center of another instructive volcanic field. The several drainage channels cut far back into the mountain mass afford a splendid opportunity to study the geologic history at first hand. Here in cross-section one can see at the base the tilted and eroded Tertiary strata upon which lie beds of consolidated ash and lava, and then on top a thin blanket of basalt. Many of the rocks exhibit remarkable examples of folding, tipping, and faulting.

In desert lands the sun, the winds, and violent rainstorms acting in conjunction with the forces of chemical decomposition are the great agencies which bring about the remarkable transformation in the landscape. All are at work scouring and shifting to bring the land to a country of flat, monotonous scenery. It is only because our deserts are, physiographically speaking, so very young that we have such varied topography, such variety of structural details.

It is always interesting to see how the different kinds of rock have yielded to the labors of these erosive agents. By reason of the difference in their habits of disintegration and their behavior under stream and sheet-flood erosion, two classes of mountain-making rocks are distinguished—granitic and nongranitic. Just as the student of trees readily distinguishes, even at a distance, the different kinds by the form of their crowns, so the student of land forms learns to discriminate between mountains made of granitic and those made of nongranitic rocks by their surface texture and their general form. Mountains of granite when attacked by erosional forces retain their steep faces until reduced to mere heaps of boulders. Nongranitic mountains, on the other hand, when wearing down, in most cases meet the detrital slopes of rock floors surrounding them in smooth concave curves, so that when seen from a distance they often assume a tentlike form.

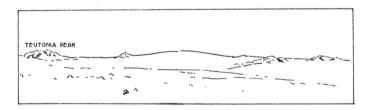

In several places the erosional forces, working away for ages at the solid, uniform-structured granite mountains, have reduced them to large-scale, convex structures of low relief known as domes. One of the most beautiful of these is the Cima dome (*cima* is Spanish for summit), seen to great advantage from the Barstow–Las Vegas highway near Valley Wells. A scenic road which begins east of Valley Wells penetrates southward through a magnificent Joshua tree forest and leads

the traveler near the broad, rounded summit and to several
remarkably fine groups of rock nubbins and residual boulders. Other similar and no less impressive features of granitic
areas are the elongated domes known as arches. One of these,
called the Cuddleback Arch and located about twenty-five
miles northwest of Barstow, presents a spectacular, rounded
crest which extends northwest-southeast for almost twenty
miles. The even contour of the arch is broken by a number of
scenic mounts; and near its northeast end is Pilot Knob, that
great landmark of the mid-Mohave Desert.

In many places where the alluvium appears to be banked
deep against mountainsides or over the ascending surfaces
of domes and arches, it forms, as above described, but a thin
cover for a low-angled slope or pediment of solid rock. A good
example of such a rock floor covered with detritus occurs to
the east of Silver Lake, where the smooth, gradual slope has,
except near the top, every appearance of being made of alluvium; yet only a few feet down is found a surface of solid
granite. The upper reaches of these pediments may be robbed
of their cover of detritus by sheet floods, and there is left only
a barren rock surface ornamented here and there by small
stones and isolated boulders.

Dry lakes or playas, also sometimes called mud flats, occupy
many of the undrained intermont basins or *bolsons* (Mexican
word for "purses") of the Mohave and Colorado deserts.

When seen from mountain elevations or airplanes they are striking features of the desert scenery. The mud-charged run-off from the bordering mountains, accumulating at the lowest point, forms ephemeral lakes, shallow but often extensive. Left to exhaustion by evaporation they soon become hard, brownish or gray, smooth-surfaced flats of clay (dry-type playa), or, if salts are present in quantity and the subsoil drainage is poor, they become pasty, more or less wet-surfaced *salinas* (wet-type playa). "They correspond," says William Foshag, "to basins that are not water-tight and those that are, and this in turn determines their efficiency in retaining the salts brought into the basin."

Desert settlers find that wells sunk in the dry-type playas sometimes yield fresh water suitable for drinking but that waters derived from the wet-type playas are generally bitter with salts. The salt-incrusted flats often remain wet or moist at the surface during most of the year, or if any parts of the areas are dry they are covered with so-called self-rising soil, a dry, powdery, puffy soil into which the traveler sometimes sinks almost to his knees. Ordinarily the apparently dry surfaces are shallow; beneath is a stratum of slimy, tenacious mud full of salts.

Rosamond and Rogers lakes, also Silver Lake and Ivanpah Lake, are typical examples of large, dry-type playas; Searles Lake, Danby and Bristol dry lakes, and Soda Lake belong to the wet class. Let the driver of a motor car beware of these dry lakes in wet weather. I have myself experienced the perils of getting mired in the slippery mud and have seen cars which were abandoned because there was no hope of getting them out before the return of dry weather.

In nature nothing is more constant than change. Just as the mountain surfaces are continually being altered by erosion, so the seemingly permanent rocks of which they are composed are breaking down under the forces of chemical decay (oxidation, hydration, carbonation, and solution) and disintegration ("physical disruption of rocks to form particles of smaller size").

Many of the rocks, though seemingly very hard, are really quite quickly worn away by running or falling sediment-bearing water. Along the deeply incised courses of the intermittent mountain streams, large pockets are hollowed out beneath the temporary cascades attending cloudburst freshets. These natural rock basins, filled with coarse gravels and sand from the torrential waters, are known as tanks or *tinajas*. They retain in the gravel interstices the purest, sweetest drinking water known to the desert traveler. Animals, such as the bighorn sheep and the ever-wise coyotes and donkeys, as well as quail and doves, possess knowledge of the presence and freshness of these reservoirs and how the waters may be tapped by digging holes and trenches in the coarse sands. Even the insects are aware of the location of these "coyote" wells, as they are often called, and several times when in need of water I have located such places by watching converging lines of thirsty bees.

It is the hard granite and nearly related rocks encircling the desert basins that furnish most of the material from which the great sand dunes are made. The sands of the Devil's Playground and of the billowy dunes near Kelso are probably derived from the nearby Granite Mountains and adjacent granitic outcrops along the Mohave River to the west.

The dunes west of Kelso and near Soda Lake, although not the most extensive, are perhaps the highest and most spectacular on the California deserts. From great distances their pure sands may be seen gleaming in the brilliant sunshine. Passengers on the Union Pacific Railroad are fortunate in passing so near them that in spring they may see the undulating surfaces carpeted with sweet-scented evening primroses, verbenas, and golden garaeas.

The impressive and stupendous Algodones Dunes of the

Colorado Desert, crossed by the highway between El Centro and Yuma, form a nearly continuous belt of northwest-trending ridges three to six miles wide and almost fifty miles long, reaching from Mammoth Station to a point below the California-Mexico boundary line near Yuma. They are made up of sands derived not only from the disintegration of the rocks of the mountains bounding the great Salton Depression but also from the breakdown of the yellowish sandstones of the old Tertiary marine beds. Just how old these dunes are no one knows; they are probably of considerable age. Their extreme narrowness and great length present several problems not easy to solve. It is possible that their original windward slope was trimmed back by vigorous wave action at a time when the water level of the Salton Sea stood much higher than it does at present. The Algodones Dunes block the drainage water from the Chocolate and Cargo Muchacho mountains to the east, and after summer cloudbursts are found small to large ponds of water which may be ephemeral or may last for a goodly number of days. Very soon after their formation, perhaps the very next day, the water may be swarming with the tadpoles of Couch's spadefoot toad.

Persons traveling to Palm Springs will do well to stop and examine the small dunes found near the Snow Creek bridge. From their peculiar form they are known as elephant-head dunes. The windward surfaces are covered with luxuriant growths of that efficient sand-catching plant, the ever-verdant epherda, or desert tea; the lee sides of many of the sand humps are barren, but from them often protrude strange proboscis-like ridges.

Important accumulations of dune sand are found also at the north end of the Maria Mountains, both at the north and at the south end of Death Valley, along the lower Amargosa River, in the Mohave River Valley northwest of Newberry, near Rogers Dry Lake, around Cadiz Dry Lake, and northeast of Twentynine Palms. A few barchanes or traveling crescentic dunes are found about four miles north of Kane Spring near the margin of the Salton Sea; also at the lower southern end of the Algondones Dunes.

Heaps of dune sand are generally related either to old lake beaches or to permanent eddies in the wind system. As an illustration of those related to beaches, the old dunes north of Rogers playa in the Mohave Desert may be mentioned. The beautiful group of dunes in Death Valley and the dunes east of Palm Springs Station on the Colorado Desert illustrate those due to peculiarities of the wind currents.

Any land area dominated by dunes should be often visited if for no other reason than to study light effects and glorious colors. Every hour of the day marks changes, and morning or evening the clean sands, viewed from a distance, are marvelously rich in translucent shades of purple, pink, blue, and yellow. Partly clouded, moonlit skies add to the effect, and under the clearing skies following rains every dune is a changing panorama of glory. Winter days near Kelso and Crucero on the Mohave Desert, at Palm Springs, and at Glamis on the Colorado Desert are never to be forgotten!

Sands, picked up and drifted along at times of severe windstorms, become one of the desert's very strongest agents of abrasion. They etch away every object with which they come in contact, not excepting the traveler's cheek and the enamel of his automobile. Nowhere is this filing action of sand in motion better exhibited than along the dry streamways of the Whitewater River on the Colorado Desert or in the lower end of Death Valley. Natural sandblasts cut the bark from all the living shrubs that have been so unfortunate as to take root there. Filing away at the rocks, they carve out the softer portions and leave the more resistant parts protruding in miniature, dikelike ridges and pinnacles.

The country to the south and west of the Salton Sea is a region dominated by bold, bare mountain forms and waterless sand and clay plains, over the surface of which are distributed innumerable odd-shaped, banded rocks which pique the curiosity of modern travelers even as they did the ancient Indians, who regarded the region as the abode of evil spirits. These rocks seem to be imitations cut in stone of every beast known and every grotesque god conceived of by ancient man. Many of them have taken on the forms of vegetables, and we often hear of fossil cabbages, turnips, and kelps brought in by the curious hunters of souvenirs who with pride pile them up in their home gardens or place them in mineral cabinets to excite the curiosity of their neighbors. The common explanation is that they are due to weathering of the iron-stained sandstones, but geologists who have studied them with care have not satisfactorily accounted for their formation. At least some of them seen to be of the nature of concretions with concentric layers of materials formed around a central core of calcite or gypsum.

In many of the brown, vegetationless, mud hills of the Carrizo region numerous plates of weathered gypsum lie exposed, many of them as flat as windowpanes and as large as dinner plates. From a considerable distance their smooth surfaces may be seen reflecting the sunlight, adding a peculiar mysteriousness to the landscape. The eroded hills have taken on queer rounded forms and some of them are highly colored. The dried mud on the surface is curiously puffed owing to the development of salt crystals which, on forming after rains, heave the clay surface upward. Similar barren, crumpled, clay hills, full of salt and gypsum, are features of the landscape near Saratoga Springs in southern Death Valley.

Desert mosaic, so-called desert pavement, is of common occurrence in the areas of igneous or volcanic rocks, though not entirely confined to these regions; limestone tracts have it too. Often over wide areas, acres in extent, the ground surface appears to have been paved with countless pebbles or small stones and rolled down to flatness with a steam roller. A creosote bush here and there is all that breaks the wide mo-

notony of the clear, tessellated rock floor. Both wind and rain
are the responsible agents. An examination of the myriads of
little flat stones will reveal that they have settled on a bed of
fine alluvium with the longest axis parallel to the ground surface, the position easiest taken when settling to rest after beating rains or winds loosen or agitate the fine soil beneath them.
These pavements make pedestrian travel difficult in summer,
because of the hard, smooth surface, and also because of the
glaring light reflected from the "varnished" rocks.

This "desert glaze" or "varnish," which makes the rocks
appear coated with oil, is common not only on pavement
pebbles but also on many of the larger rock surfaces in all
arid countries. It has long been thought to be solely due to
the slow deposition of certain soluble constituents which have
been drawn to the surface of the rocks by the sun's rays. But
it has recently been shown that lichens growing on rocks
having a manganese and iron content may also be active
agents in the formation of desert varnish. (See page 153.)

In masses of conglomerate rocks found on the desert slope
of the San Gabriel Mountains and considered to have been
formed in Eocene times are embedded rocks with brown and
black coatings of desert varnish, showing that arid conditions
favorable to the deposition of desert varnish existed even in
those ancient times.

It is pertinent now to mention some of the notable fossil-
bearing rocks of our desert region. Here we have a sequence
of deposits representing many ages.

In the Marble Mountains of the eastern Mohave Desert are
excellent Lower and Middle Cambrian rocks, the most west-
erly Cambrian sedimentaries with fossils in the desert. In
abundance are trilobites, pelagic gastropods, and lingulid
brachiopods. Showing up also in this same general area in
beautiful sequence are other Paleozoic fossiliferous formations (Ordovician, Silurian, Devonian, and Permian).

In the Kingston and Nopah mountain limestones there is a sequence of fossils representing materials of the ancient Cordilleran geosyncline, really a broad trough of marine deposits. Here fossil marine invertebrates are common.

Deposits of triassic gastropods have been located in the Soda Mountains near Baker Dry Lake; also in the Panamint Mountains to the north.

Jurassic and Cretaceous fossil-bearing formations are not represented, since those were times of metamorphosis and mountain uplift rather than of subsidence and deposition.

In the Paso Mountains the early Tertiary (Paleocene) is represented by sparse remains of mammals, fish, crocodiles, and river turtles.

In the Titus Canyon Formation of mid-Tertiary (Oligocene) red sandstones east of Death Valley some earlier larger mammal remains occur. Included are a primitive camel, a small horse, and several rodents. Titanotherium, a rhinoceros-like animal, with heavy flattened skull and two divergent hornlike protuberances, was discovered. Examples of all these interesting fossil beasts are shown in the Pacific Coast Borax Company's Death Valley Museum and in the Death Valley National Monument Museum at the Visitor's Center.

A number of basins developed in middle and late Miocene times, and among known sediments laid down in them are those of the Mud Hills of the Barstow Formation. These rocks can be traced from the Black Mountains north of Hinkley to the Calico Mountains north of Daggett. The fossils unearthed here give us a good idea of the abundance of life in Miocene times. So far there have been discovered the remains of three-toed horses, camels, pronghorns, and a small mastodon; among the carnivores were cats, dogs, and weasels. Some of these animals in altered form have persisted to the present day.

In the Calico Mountains are lacustrine deposits contain-

ing claylike nodules in which are centrally buried castings
in silicon of numerous small insects, most of them in an extraordinary state of preservation.

The Pliocene is best represented in the Ricardo Formation
of Red Rock Canyon. Its animal fossils are similar to those of
the Miocene fauna near Barstow except that the animals are
more like modern forms and tell a story of gradual evolution.
Horses, camels, large carnivores, rodents, rabbits, lizards, and
birds have been found.

South of Owens Lake in the Coso Range, the late Pliocene
sediments give us a zebralike horse, suggesting that horses
passed through a zebrine phase. There is also a camel larger
than any of our modern camels.

There are many late Pleistocene deposits in the Mohave
Desert's old lake beds. The lakes themselves, of which Lake
Manix (see pp. 112, 116) is a good example, were formed in
glacial times of abundant rains and also snow in the higher
surrounding mountains (San Gabriels and San Bernardinos).
The fauna was very diverse and included large and small
horses, bisons, camels, bear, the dire wolf, pond turtles (*Clem-
mys*); also the desert tortoise. The Mohave chub (*Gila mohavensis*) is there as well as a variety of small snails (fresh
water) and a remarkably rich bird fauna, including flamin-
gos, ducks, cormorants, pelicans, and grebes. Land birds are
represented by an eagle and the great horned owl.

All these fossil forms have been studied by Dr. Hildegard
Howard of the Los Angeles County Museum, and reconstruc-
tions are artfully exhibited in the Museum's hall of fossils.

Fossiliferous deposits at or near the surface of the Colorado
Desert are well known. The oldest are of the Cenozoic (Pleistocene) Age. Such are those of Indio and the Mecca Mud
Hills, which have yielded fossil horses and camels. Other
similar sediments found in the Anza-Borrego area have recently received much attention. The fauna represented is
rich indeed. Some late Pliocene marine invertebrates repre-

sented in the Imperial Formation are to be found in the bizarre Split Mountain area of the Anza-Borrego State Park.

Marine deposits of late Pliocene and later Pleistocene tell us of inundations of waters of the Gulf of California as far north as the San Gorgonio Pass. Here exhibited is a gulf fauna (barnacles, corals, sand dollars, oysters, etc.) with Caribbean elements suggesting that in Tertiary times there was a connection between the Caribbean Sea and the Pacific Ocean. There are some interesting Pliocene marine deposits in the bluffs along the Colorado River as far north as Parker Dam. There is some additional evidence, including deposits revealed by deep borings, that the northward invasion of the Gulf of California may have reached as far as the Cadiz-Danby area.

Marine Eocene (probably middle Eocene) sediments show up in the Orocopia Mountains east of the Salton Sea in a band running across the range in a northwest-southeast direction. It is a shallow-water fauna (mollusca and foraminifera) that is found. The only other middle Eocene in southern California is in the Santa Monica Mountains near the Pacific Coast.

4. Weather and Climatic Features

If we are so fortunate as to visit our deserts during several successive seasons or over a period of years, we soon discover that there is a well-defined desert climate, with four seasons climatologically as well as biologically well marked. The transition from one season to another in these semitropical deserts is usually gradual, much more so than in deserts farther to the north and more inland. Nowhere do we see here the abruptness of seasonal changes so characteristic of the Gobi and other deserts of central Asia.

It is largely due to winds that deserts are made (see page 2), and winds constitute one of the desert's most interesting weather phenomena. On our California deserts the summer winds, though warm, are usually moderate, but in winter and spring the air currents push with much vigor. Winds from the northeast, known as Santa Anas when they reach the southern Californian coast, are the worst, and at times reach velocities of forty miles or more an hour. They often come on with extraordinary abruptness following rainstorms; being very dry, they quickly dissipate the moisture-bearing clouds.*

* The air of the Santa Anas is warmed by compressional heating and becomes very dry. Since the air currents are descending, turbulence or vertical convection, so essential to cloud formation, ceases.

Their maximum strength is attained soon after sunrise. Picking up fine particles of soil on dry lake basins and dunes, they fill the atmosphere with dust clouds, furiously lash the vegetation, and set every insecure thing on the move. These are the winds that cause prospectors to put all sorts of curious braces on their shanties and to double-nail the sideboards and shingles. If caught while camping out, they must weigh down with rocks everything from tarpaulins to dishpans. The wind usually drops at sunset and the nights are then surprisingly calm: the red skies of sunset change to clear blue-black and sparkle with myriads of brilliant stars. The smoke of the campfire now ascends straight up.

I once had on the deserts of western Nevada an unnerving experience with the winds that left on my mind an image so vivid that it can never be effaced. It was in the month of March. All day I had labored against a strong southwest wind that was prophetic of soaking rains. Sure enough, before night the precipitation came, but it was in the form of snow. I found shelter in a miner's cabin, put a pot of beans on the stove to cook, and went to bed, expecting at daybreak to waken and find myself snowed in for at least one or two days. With a suddenness that was startling, the wind at nine o'clock veered squarely to the north and began blowing with a hurricane violence that set every timber in the little shanty creaking and groaning. Though the house was well braced, it seemed every minute that it must go. There was nothing to do but wait under cover, for it would have been little better than suicide to venture out of doors. The eerie effect was heightened by the continuous, thunderous roar, and the angry wind continued unabated until near daybreak.

Violent north winds, sometimes also called Santa Anas, are usually of only a few days' duration. The strong winds that blow with most protracted violence are those that come in from the Pacific Coast, hailing the approach of winter rains. Nimbus clouds and lenticular clouds, appearing like great

Zeppelins over the western mountains, are heralds of their oncoming. The clouds continue beating their way in, often seemingly against odds, until at length they cover the skies. Then silence comes and the rain descends, at first gently, but steadily increasing to a downpour. The stronger the initial winds, the better the chances for precipitation.

During the months of April and May, when fog is commonest on the Coast, the period of violent sand and dust storms comes to the upper Colorado Desert, especially in the San Gorgonio Pass* and along the course of the Whitewater River to the Salton Sea. It is these winds sweeping in from the Coast that, picking up the sands, and often pebbles as large as peas, etch the windshields and painted surfaces of motor cars, blind the traveler's eyes with dust, and cause him many unhappy hours. It is wise, especially if one has a camper or house-trailer, to avoid desert travel when the coastal fogs of spring are on. But there is always something deeply and highly exciting in the sounds of these storms, particularly in the singing of the wind-driven sands, and I have many times purposely pushed out on foot into them to hear the wild music.

A wind known as the "evening blow" is common in summer. It is probably a local adjustment phenomenon. It arises about sundown and is a strong, steady west wind that does much to drive out the heated air of the long days and temper

* Few people recognize what a great draught channel the San Gorgonio Pass is. As W. P. Blake long ago pointed out, through it the air pours "from the ocean to the interior with peculiar uniformity and persistence, thus supplying the partial vacuum caused by the ascent of heated air from the surface of the parched plains and deserts." The wind "is not an ordinary shifting breeze, but is a constant, powerful current of air sweeping through the pass from the west. It pours from the Pacific in an apparently unbroken, unvarying stream, passing over the surface with such violence that all the fine grains of sand are lifted from the dry channels of the streams and are driven along the descending slopes until they find a final resting-place to the leeward of the projecting spurs" of San Jacinto.

the weather for those who must live continuously in the interior regions. The average velocity is not great, about twenty miles an hour. It may continue well through the night but always drops before sunrise. It is best observed in long, troughlike depressions such as the Salton Sink, although the Mohavean mesas and interior basins get their share too.

Whirlwinds or tornillos are commonest on calm summer and autumn afternoons when all the air is shimmering with heat. They are caused by the local heating of the air above the flat desert floor. During this period of seasonal calms there is generally at midday a lack of wind velocity sufficient to act as an impetus for any heat adjustment of the ordinary kind, and so it has to take place in the form of "explosions" or "leaks." As a result, swiftly rising columns of expanding air are formed. Currents of surface air move in to replace the air that is rising, and a whirl is developed. Gathering up sand and dust and bits of dried vegetation, the dust devil, as it is sometimes called, now begins to move slowly across the land, gathering momentum and gaining in height as it goes forward. Sometimes half a dozen or more of these wandering dust whirls, some of them a thousand feet high, are visible at one time. Watched from mountain tops, the slender chimneys of ascending dust are imposing and fascinating sights. On our southern California deserts they seldom assume destructive proportions, but in some of the broad Old World deserts they develop into violent storms.

The desert rains of the autumn, winter, and spring season are of the Pacific marine type. They come for the most part from the west and southwest. Energetic storms with high fronts then climb the Sierra and other coastal mountains, reaching not only the immediate desert but far out across the Great Basin states of Nevada and Utah. Drenching rains of this type may occur as early as mid-October but are seldom experienced later than the first of April. The winter maximum of the Pacific Coast area asserts itself all over southern

California and the interior deserts in January and February. The winter and spring quota of rainfall, where local conditions such as the altitude of mountain ranges do not increase it, progressively diminishes northeastward from the desert's western edge.

One of the pleasantest times to visit the desert is during periods when winter rains occur. Indeed, incoming rain clouds are generally for me the signal to start desertward. Let me have the delicious odors of the creosote bush and the saltbush when they are wetted with gentle rains, look upon the endless variety and beauty of the clouds' far-flung forms, have the silence of the uninhabited mesas, and I am in a land enchanted.

The higher mountains are often whitened by midwinter snows; some of them, such as Telescope Peak in the Panamint Mountains and Charleston Peak in the Spring Mountains of southwestern Nevada, may receive generous amounts and carry snow patches until midsummer. Most of the other ranges receive only temporary coverings, which last for periods of but a few days to several weeks. One of the most fascinating sights of winter is the entire Mohave Desert blanketed with snow. At such times the individualization and varied configuration of the lost ranges are brought out in a way that is very marked. As you view these whitened highlands you feel indeed that you are in a new land of mystery, for "the tentlike mountains gleam like the encampment of some mighty host." On the high Mohave Desert, one may reasonably expect to experience a light fall of snow any time after the middle of November and as late as mid-April.

Not much is known concerning the humidity of desert areas. In general it may be said that in the open desert there is a large relative fluctuation. It is low at midday and relatively high at night, the greatest and most rapid alternations occurring in summer. It must always be kept in mind that the desert is very much the domain of sun and wind. Rain and snow are among its most infrequent phenomena. Day after day the sun beats down upon the barren soil, and the drying winds are seldom idle. All places get rain at some time, but hundreds of days often pass without a drop.

The summer rains of the desert are of the Gulf type. Water vapor is borne from the Gulf of California by southerly winds. Clouds soon form and bank up high over the heated interior basins. Much of this summer rainfall is spotted. It occurs on hot, quiet days and consists of cloudbursts, or heavy showers of short duration. These brief rains are usually accompanied by high, gusty winds carrying great clouds of dust. Precipitation may be of two or more inches in a short half-hour, producing what are known as sheet-floods. The waters gather together in the "oueds" or dry drainage channels, and on their onward march become freighted with sand, boulders, and loosened trees and shrubs, which they carry down to the lower levels with a roar that may be audible, at least in the hush following the storm, for miles around. Woe to the foolish camper who has made his temporary home on the sands of the washes down which the waters rush! Pots, pans, and all his belongings, including his automobile, may be caught up in the swirling floods and come to a sad end.

The waters from these heavy rains run off so quickly that most of the desert vegetation profits little from them. Only the plants that live in the washes get a chance for a real drink. Among the curiosities encountered by the desert traveler are the local bits of verdure marking the courses of streamways that carry the flood waters. On the whole these torrents are very destructive to both plants and animals. Mice and other small burrowing animals are the greatest sufferers.

The hottest days of summer occur when low-pressure areas move in from the Coast and form immediately over the Great Basin. Then not only do desert dwellers swelter in the torrid heat* but also the inhabitants of the cities of the coastal strip. It must not be inferred that days of unfavorably high tem-

---

* Summer shade temperatures of 105° to 118° F. are frequent. The highest recorded shade temperature, 134° F., is from Death Valley.

peratures are far greater in number on the desert than at many points on the coastal side of the mountains. Cool days of summer on the Coast are matched by tolerably pleasant, though not as cool, weather on the desert. This is especially true of the Mohave Desert. Travelers will find it well to keep this in mind when beginning summer journeys involving desert travel in the daytime. It is really surprising how many days are agreeable and during how many nights a blanket is required for sleeping comfort.

The Colorado Desert owes much of its winter climatic excellence to its lack of snow and to the clear skies, ideal temperatures, and highly invigorating daily changes. The midday sun is delightfully warm and the night temperatures seldom bring frost. Winter days on the Mohave Desert are often equally pleasant and stimulating, but owing to the higher altitudes the nights are much cooler and over much of the region chilly temperatures and hard frosts are the rule. David G. Thompson records the average length of the growing season for crop plants at ten chosen stations on the Mohave Desert as 257 days. The average length of the growing season for cultivated crops at Indio in the Salton Sink may be placed at almost 365 days. The Colorado Desert's record for warm winter days is matched on the Mohave Desert only at Bagdad.

Considerable daily range in temperature is experienced in the climate of all great deserts, but it is well to remember that our Western North American deserts, because of their proximity to the regulating waters of the sea, are not subject to the daily extremes of heat and cold encountered in the interior of the great Palearctic deserts of Africa and Asia, where temperature ranges as great as 68° F. (from 31° to 99° F.) have been known within twenty-four hours. David G. Thompson, speaking of this temperature fluctuation on the Mohave Desert, says: "In summer the temperature frequently falls from above 100° in the daytime to below 75° or 70° at night, and in winter it frequently rises from below the freezing-point in the early mornings to 65° or 70° at midday. The daily range is probably a little less in winter than in summer."

The intensity of aridity in desert lands is perhaps best expressed by what is known as the evaporation-rainfall ratio. It is the ratio between possible evaporation and actual rainfall, and it shows the discrepancy between the water upon which plants can draw and the desiccating effect of the desert climate and sun.

"It is," says Buxton, "of very great interest to biologists, and it is probably one of the most important factors in determining whether a place will or will not be desert. So far as we know it is high in all desert regions, and it is not high in regions which are not desert. In an unusually dry year the evaporation-rainfall ratio will be vastly increased, so that, at a time when the mere drought is pressing hardly on flora and fauna, an increased discrepancy between rainfall and evaporation is thrown into the scale against them."

Observations to determine the possible evaporation have been made at several points in the American and in the Palearctic deserts. Pans and tanks of water were placed where they got the full play of sun and wind. The annual evaporation of Harold Reservoir (Mohave Desert) was found to be about 87 inches, that at Pahrump about 85 inches, that at Yuma about 100 inches, that at Tucson, Arizona, about 90 inches, and that at Cahuilla about 116 inches. In some parts of the Libyan Desert, where rain falls only once in every four or five years, the total of possible evaporation is believed to be close to 150 inches a year.

5. Insects and Other Invertebrates

The number of species of insects in any region as large as the one under consideration is so great that only a few of those most conspicuous in form and most interesting in their habits can be considered. As the specialized biology of these arid-region insects is unraveled they become more and more fascinating creatures for investigation. I find that their collection and study is one of the greatest sources of travel delight.

The most interesting question is concerned with the manner in which the desert insects manage to pull themselves through the times of summer heat and dryness or the long, protracted droughts when, for several seasons or even years, there is little or no food available for either larvae or adults. The question has been answered for the butterflies and moths, and it is quite possible that the way to a similar answer has been pointed out for most of the other insect groups. It is now known that when inimical conditions press hard upon the larval butterflies and moths they stop feeding and go into a kind of summer sleep, called aestivation, hiding the while under leaves and stones. There they lie in dormancy perhaps for months or years, until a fortunate season arrives. Then, immediately alert to the favorable conditions, they resume their normal life history. When in the pupal state they may again go into a long period of rest, some of them waiting two years or more before emerging.

Dr. P. A. Buxton has divided insects into two types, the "spenders" and the "savers," with a series of intermediates. The "spenders" he designates as those of damp climates which eat food of high water content. They practice no economy of water but pass it freely in their excreta and feces and possibly through the body wall as well. To the second group belong the majority of insects living on deserts. Their food is dry and many of them withstand long starvation, living for months in parched sand without food or drink. Several kinds of water economy are practiced by these "savers." Some are almost proof against loss of water from the body surfaces; they excrete their uric acid in a solid state and extract water from the contents of the hind gut so that the feces pass dry. Others, subject to loss of water through evaporation, burn fat at a rate sufficient to replace it.

When burning heat and lack of food kill the adult insects, their eggs may be the means of continuing the life of the species. These eggs, like the seeds of many plants, tolerating great dryness and in some cases the actual loss of water by the embryo itself, hatch only when moistened by the rains that end the dry spells. Eggs of springtails, normally hatching in 8 or 10 days, have been known, when dried, to live 271 days without dying. Eggs of one of the South African locusts, which in moist soils hatch in 14 days in summer, may remain alive in very dry soil for more than three years.

Under rocks and among dry sticks and leaves, the color of which they resemble to a remarkable degree, live those primitive, mottled-gray insects, the fishmoths or bristletails (*Thysanura*). They seem to mind neither the ovenlike air nor the dryness, but they avoid the direct sunlight. These insects have protrusible vesicles on the abdominal segments and it has been suggested that these serve for absorption of water and therefore that the insects can take advantage of dew or other moisture when it is available.

The great order *Orthoptera,* which includes grasshoppers, crickets, walking-sticks, and katydids, is well represented by numbers of specialized forms. Dr. Morgan Hebard brings out the interesting fact that many of the desert grasshoppers have habits so individual that once we know these habits in connection with the exact locality where the insects live we may proceed at once to an identification without further aid. Specimens from one locality may look very much like those from another and still be widely different in habits. Bruner's silver-spotted grasshopper (*Bootettix argentatus*), with wings a rich green, spotted with brown and mother-of-pearl, is one of the handsomest insects of the desert. It lives exclusively on the creosote bush, never resting on the ground. If driven out it flies immediately to another creosote bush. It is certainly a good example of a creature of restricted habitat. In the month of June I have found the young, pale-green, wingless forms lined up by the thousands on the slender, gray, woody stems. The ghostly grayish grasshopper that flies in undulations before you in Death Valley is *Anconia integra,* but in that region it is much more pallid than elsewhere. In late April and May, grasshoppers are frequently very plentiful on the Mohave Desert. They fly up in crackling clouds before the automobile moving slowly along the winding desert roads. By hundreds they jump into the driver's seat and make such a rattling noise as they strike the windshield and the sides of the car that one may easily imagine he is in a hailstorm.

The unique sand-treader crickets of the genera *Ammobaetes* and *Macrobaetes* are small, pale tan-colored insects with black eyes and special adaptations of combs of long hairs on the lower hind legs to enable them to make sure progress in sand. They lie buried during the day and emerge at night, especially on warm summer nights.

In Imperial Valley and about Yuma the Mexican ground

cricket (*Acheta similis*) becomes a real pest in summer. Its persistent, pulsating chirp is one of the most familiar night sounds of that part of the desert. These crickets get into houses and eat clothing and are continually being trampled under foot. On several occasions strong winds have been known to carry swarms of them far to the northeastward into the higher desert valleys. Most of the little native vegetation that was green was entirely consumed by their greedy jaws.

Capribotes sp. is the name of a very rare newly discovered carnivorous katydid, gray-brown and brown spotted, whose forelegs are strongly toothed to aid in grasping its prey, generally a noctuid moth. These insects will come to an artificial light but are never seen in the daytime. The female has an enormous ovipositor.

There are a number of small, delicately colored green-and-tan cockroaches that live on the sand dunes. The sand cockroach (*Arenivaga*) is very common. They are handsome creatures, bearing little resemblance to the large non-native "roaches" that inhabit the kitchens of public eating places. We generally see them at night while we are out observing with the aid of our flashlights.

Very curious are the queer, earthen shelter-galleries built over dead desert shrubs by the Arizona desert termite (*Amitermes arizonensis*). Often the interior wood is almost entirely eaten away, leaving fragile earthen tubes which crumble to dust upon being touched. The insects are most active after summer rains, and at such times almost all the dead shrubs over wide areas may appear like plants "spattered thick with mud." Four other species of "desert termites" (*Amitermes*) are found living in the bases of agaves, and in the trunks of desert willow, ironwood, cholla, and ocotillo, but these build no extensive mudtubes. The black-legged termite (*Reticulotermes tibialis*) occurs along the western border of the Colorado and Mohave deserts under stones and dead logs, in dead wood and cow chips. The fact that the body of this insect is wholly black illustrates the folly of calling all termites "white ants." One interesting point about termites is the fact that almost all the species have, in their intestinal tract, thousands of tiny, one-celled parasites, known as flagellate protozoans. They depend on these for the digestion of the cellulose of the dry wood they eat. The protozoans are equally dependent upon their termite hosts. This interdependence is generally so marked that the termites die if freed of the protozoans and thé protozoans die if deprived of their wood diet. It has been shown that the desert termites of the genus *Amitermes* are different from all other termite relatives, for they seem to get on perfectly well without their protozoan helpers. Just why, no one seems to know.

Most of the desert's tiny thrips are host-specific, each kind feeding only on a particular host plant. Thus the thrip living on cheesebush will not feed on the sap of indigo bush and the one on coldenia will not live on brittlebush. One of the most interesting thrips is found only in the grooves of the corrugated leaves of *Coldenia plicata* and peculiarly only on those plants that occur on sand dunes. Another rare black thrip mimics the ant both in form and in actions. One of the haplothrips living on *Coldenia palmeri* is very tolerant of heat, being an active feeder even when the near-ground air temperature runs up to 130° F.

Strong of wing, the keen-eyed dragonflies make their way far from the water holes where their eggs are laid and the nymphs develop. It seems almost an anomaly that these insects, which we always associate with water, should at times hunt their insect prey twenty or even thirty miles from the nearest known springs or streams, but seeing them do so is an experience frequent enough on deserts.

In the fine sands, and in the powdery soils that floor the shallow caves, we regularly see the queer, conical pits made by ant lion larvae to snare their prey. The desert's ant population is so considerable that the rapacious larvae of these insects always find plenty to eat. The gray-winged adult ant lions are among the most persistent of the insects that collect about lights on a summer evening. The family to which these insects belong is particularly well represented in arid regions of many parts of the world.

It must be pointed out that there are certain robust long-legged snipe flies (*Rhagionidae*) whose larvae also make conical pits in dust and, like the ant lion larvae, feed on ants. They are only rarely found but it is a real discovery when you do find them. The adult flies are called snipe flies because they have a long snipelike proboscis which inflicts a painful bite.

The most remarkable scale insect of the desert area appears to be the creosote bush lac-scale (*Tachardiella larreae*). For many of the scales, high temperatures and marked dryness are the greatest deterrents to existence. But here is one that not only tolerates heat but thrives on it.* The lac insects, crowded on the stems of the creosote bush, hide beneath warty coverings of dirty-brown or reddish resinous material. This resin was once valuable to the Indians, who used it as a mending material for their vessels. The oak wax scale (*Cerococcus quercus*) lives on the scrub oaks of the desert mountains; its waxy coverings are bright yellow and give a curious warty appearance to the branches bearing the closely crowded insects. I once heard that the Indians used this wax for chewing gum, and out of curiosity I tried the golden sweetmeat, but found the nasty paste dreadfully bitter, indeed as unpalatable as wormwood. It is probable that had I persisted the end-product might have been better, but I did not then have, nor have I now, the courage to stay with the ordeal to its possible pleasant end.

* Another coccid remarkably adapted to aridity is *Margarodes vitium*, which occurs in arid parts of South America. At the end of larval growth it becomes completely covered with a waxy coating and is then known as the "ground pearl." In this condition it can resist prolonged drying. When the cyst is put into damp soil it absorbs moisture and continues its development. Professor G. F. Ferris of Stanford University found one of these sand pearls alive after seventeen years in a museum case!

The true bugs live on plant juices or on the blood of animals. The period of activity of these insects must in most cases necessarily coincide with the period of active plant growth. Following the advent of spring flowers they are seen everywhere and may continue to be found late in summer if any of the plants such as the wild buckwheats (*Eriogonum*) continue to grow. An examination of the tree yuccas in late March and early April will reveal enormous numbers of the prettily marked lateral leafhopper (*Oncometopius lateralis*) swarming over the leaves. They hang on so tight that it is necessary to shake the branches vigorously to get them off.

In summer large broods of the apache cicada (*Diceroprocta apache*) appear in the Salton Basin and all through the day one hears their continuous *zing*. Often the mad chorus continues long after sunset. All during the sunny hours, while the cicadas are busiest singing, the great cicada killer (*Sphecius convallis*), a robust wasp with brown and yellow bands, is fiendishly at work bringing in cicadas as her victims to provide food for her larvae. The paralyzed insects are stored in burrows made in the soil and on them the eggs of the wasp are laid.

Bold asilid or robber flies are frequently seen resting on the ground or darting about while carrying away, like hawks, their insect victims. A great, brown, hairy species of robust form, *Rhapionidas xanthos,* should be looked for emerging from sands and gravels in the high desert valleys in May. It belongs to a family of flies, species of which are very rare, though widely distributed in both hemispheres. The commonest desert asilid is a large gray species belonging to the genus *Erax*.

Various biting midges (*Chironomidae*) from salt and brackish waters of deserts are known throughout the world. These are the little black flies (e.g., *Leptonops kerteszi* var. *americanus*) that swarm so persistently about one's face on warm and stuffy evenings. They are exceptionally annoying on account of their fierce bites. They should not be confused with

Hippaletes flaviceps, the salute fly so annoying in the Coachella Valley, which, after years of search, was found to pupate and to breed in decaying vegetation. Ephydrid or saltmarsh flies (*Ephydra hians* and *E. subopaca*) are found almost everywhere about salt and alkaline streams and lakes. The waters of Owens Lake and the brackish pools in Death Valley and the Salton Sink are at times teeming with the larvae. These, each about 12 mm. long, wiggle about in the almost syrupy briny or brackish waters and exhibit their remarkable anal breathing tubes and their curious hooked legs, by means of which they often attach themselves to the bottom rocks. The Piute Indians are said to have collected and dried these larvae for food. That any living creature should be able to find a favorable environment in the concentrated salt waters is most remarkable. Pupation takes place beneath the water. The adults escape from the pupal case and are carried to the surface in a bubble of air. In these same brackish pools may sometimes be found the larvae of the great buzzing horsefly (*Tabanus punctifer*), soldier flies (*Stratiomyidae*), water boatmen (*Corixidae*), and several small hydrophilid beetles whose life histories are imperfectly known.

As a rule, desert areas in the natural state are quite free from mosquitoes, but with the introduction of irrigation and the creation of many permanent and transient pools where their larvae may feed, mosquitoes become increasingly abundant. Forty years ago when camping widely over the Salton Basin my night's sleep was seldom menaced by a mosquito, but now almost anywhere in the Valley a good night's rest in the open is impossible, even during the middle of the winter months. The Mohave Desert is as a whole still sufficiently dry to ensure freedom from mosquito bites in most situations. The mosquito prevailing throughout the Imperial Valley is *Culex quinquefasciatus,* a common house mosquito of tropical and subtropical countries of the world. It breeds throughout the year in water holes, particularly polluted ones, wayside pools, and ditches. Winds often carry the adults far from their breeding places, and this fact probably accounts for their wide distribution in waterless areas. *Anopheles pseudopunctipennis,* a malarial mosquito, is known to breed in roadside ditches near Thermal but is not here believed to be a carrier of disease. The larvae of *Theobaldia inornata* have been collected in the waters of many pools of the desert area. The adults, large mosquitoes with a persistent, low hum, often gather in disconcerting numbers about the camp at night.

Those specialized mosquitoes of the genus *Psorophora,* frequent enough in northern Mexico, may yet be found with us, since they are peculiarly adapted to desert conditions. The eggs, protected by tough spiny coats, are deposited singly in the bottoms of rain pools and may lie dormant for months or years awaiting their immersion in some transient pond formed by the infrequent rains. Upon hatching, the wrigglers pass through their life history in a very few days. The adults emerge as metallic insects of spidery appearance and vicious bite.

The coleoptera or beetles are among the most conspicuous of insects. Of these the darkling beetles of the genus *Eleodes* are particularly successful inhabitants of deserts, in both the Old World and the New. Contrary to the general law of desert animal coloration, the many species of *Eleodes* have bodies colored for the most part a deep black. This makes them very conspicuous and, in addition, subject to the maximum of heat absorption. Not only have they the sun beating down upon them but also they get the full effect of reflection from the hot earth beneath them. We probably have little appreciation of what high temperatures exist right down next to the ground surface where they crawl. The amazing thing is that we often find them active during the hottest parts of the day as well as in the cooler hours of the night. Dr. Buxton has shown that these beetles may obtain a considerable amount of water by eating fragments of organic matter which

Slow-flowing Amargosa River southeast of Death Valley.
The plants growing along its salt-incrusted margin are saltbushes.

Howard H. Bliss

Blue palo verde (*Cercidium floridum*) growing in rocky gorge of the Chocolate Mountains of the Colorado Desert.

Mountains of dark red volcanic rocks with talus, forming steep bajadas at their base. Most of the plants growing in the sandy wash are hymenoclea bushes. A smoke tree on the right frames the picture.

N. Curtis Armstrong

Limestone caverns of great beauty are found in Providence Mountains
of the eastern Mohave Desert. Long stalactites hang from the roof
of this one in Mitchel's Caverns, now a state park.

Pink-flowered desert willows fringe the borders of a Colorado Desert wash.

Near Cima in the eastern Mohave Desert is the largest stand of yuccas in the United States. The short-leaved, slender-trunked yucca was named *Yucca brevifolia Jaegeriana* in reference to the author's contribution to desert plant knowledge.

Fine specimen of Mohave yucca. Growing at its base are a barrel cactus and a deerhorn cactus.

Beautiful specimens of Weber Joshua tree (*Yucca brevifolia weberi*). North slopes of San Bernardino Mountains.

Beautiful erosional forms occur where rain and wind have
sculptured the clays and sandstone deposits of ancient lakes.

Beautiful eroded granites in Joshua Tree National Monument.
The larger shrubs are mostly cat's-claw and blackbrush.

Crescentic dunes or barchans of the Colorado Desert. The shrub
in the foreground is one of the saltbushes (*Atriplex*).

The Pinnacles near Trona, thought to have been formed by blue-green
algae around the vents of hot springs issuing from the floor of a
large fresh-water lake that once covered the area.

Picturesque sand dunes near Stovepipe Wells in **Death Valley.**

The desert tortoise found amidst a field of the beautiful yellow California malacothrix. Note the handsomely marked angular plates of the tortoise shell or carapace.

Howard H. Bliss

Creosote bush grows in almost pure stands in the broad Pinto Basin in the southern section of the Joshua Tree National Monument. Pinto Mountains in background.

A wet-type desert dry-lake. The water is found just a few feet, maybe only inches, below. Plants in distance are those of salt-tolerant Allenrolfia.

Young of the house finch, which is an early nester on our deserts.

Couch's spade-foot toad
in its burrow far beneath
the surface of the soil.
It was exposed by digging.

Lon McClanahan

Antelope ground squirrel,
sprightly denizen of the
desert's brush and rocky
areas.

Avery Edwin Field

Bobcats frequent the desert
foothill areas. They are
adept hunters and swift
runners for short distances.

Edmund C. Jaeger

Sand and gravel crater
of one of the desert
harvester ants. Some of
these craters measure
a foot across and are
six inches high.

Edmund C. Jaeger

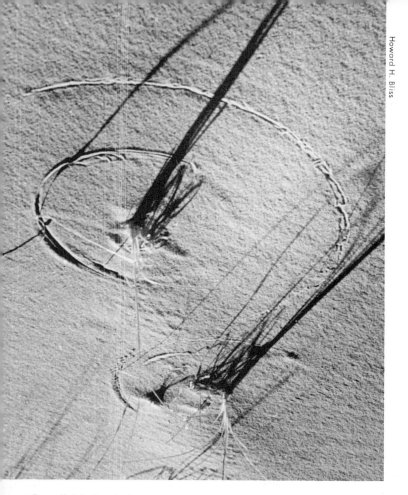

Howard H. Bliss

Beautiful designs in dune
sand made by long-leaved
grasses blown by the wind.

Edmund C. Jaeger

Usually the barrel cactus
grows as a single tall plant
but this is a cluster of
thirty-two, an unusual
phenomenon.

Fine specimen of deerhorn cactus (*Opuntia echinocarpa*) in the Joshua Tree National Monument. Joshua tree in the background

The parasitic *Pilostyles thurberi* is the smallest flowering plant in the world. Each of the small dark "kernels" found on the branches of Emory's Dalea is a separate plant.

The desert fan palm (*Washingtonia filifera*) is peculiarly almost wholly a Colorado Desert tree. It occurs in small groups in oases and canyons.

Sand verbena scents the air in spring on the Colorado Desert.

Desert bighorns, female *(left)*, ram and young female *(right)* on rocky slopes of the Desert Game Refuge, Sheep Mountains, Nevada.

The magnificent smoke tree grows in the broad sand washes
of the hot southern desert.

have absorbed water from the atmosphere in the evening when dew is forming. He has also shown that such insects can keep their temperature slightly lower than that of their environment, presumably by evaporating water during the daytime. These beetles, known to the traveler as circus bugs because of the singular habit of standing on their heads with the tip of the abdomen thrust upward, are vegetarians, and often they visit the nests of harvester ants to feed on the fragmental remains of seeds and flowers which lie about the ant hills. In spring and early summer, which is their period of migration, they are found in great numbers.

Very common on sunny days is the sand dune beetle *Eusattus,* one of the darkling beetles. It crawls about vigorously, leaving very characteristic long trails. The small, round, high-arched body, about one-third of an inch long, is light brown and has a very definite band of golden hairs on the last segment of the thorax.

The boring beetles (*Buprestridae*) and their larvae play a major part in reducing the dying vegetation to powder, and here perform the work done by the bacteria of more humid countries. Once wood is dead, it rapidly goes to pieces under their labors. Some of their activities are mentioned in connection with the desert trees (see pp. 174, 175, 178, 182).

The wealth of unusual species and the abundance of individuals of strange form among the meloid beetles make their collection an exciting experience. The flowers of the late-blooming composites, such as the scale broom and the rabbit brush, often teem with them. They seem particularly fond of the flowers of the evening primroses and at times reduce great fields of them to bare stems in a few days. There is one particularly large species, *Lytta magister,* with red head and thorax and black, pitted wing-covers, which at times occur in such numbers on the gravelly mesas that a rasping sound fills the air about them. This noise is made by the scraping of the hard wing-covers against stones and dead

vegetation as the beetles crawl awkwardly over the ground.
I have found that the amber-colored blood of this insect is
highly irritating when applied to the skin and will produce
blisters in a few minutes. The greedy larvae probably feed on
the eggs of grasshoppers.

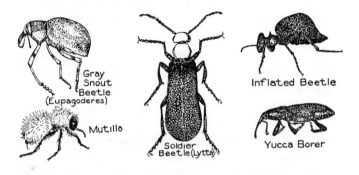

Gray
Snout
Beetle
(Eupagoderes)

Mutilla

Soldier
Beetle (Lytta)

Inflated Beetle

Yucca Borer

The inflated beetle (*Cysteodemus armatus*), with much-
arched wing-covers, crawls among the flowers and adorns itself with yellow pollen. This often completely fills the pits in
the wing-covers, and one is tempted to think some protection
is gained by this camouflage. We frequently see lone individuals on the sands, bustling about with all the appearance of
being in a dreadful hurry and about to impart some important news to their fellows.

The majority of desert bees are solitary species which make
cells of resin and sand, which they mount on shrubs; or they
construct nests in burrows excavated by themselves or found
as natural cavities in the soil. The cells are provisioned with
a paste made of pollen and nectar, and on this the eggs are
laid. The time of emergence of the young bees is remarkably
synchronized with the blooming of the particular flowers on
which they feed and there is thus a distinct succession of
species with the advance of the floral season. The same moisture that stimulates plant growth initiates the development
of the bees. Sometimes when rains are not favorable the larvae

do not complete their development, and there are indications that under these conditions they may hold over in the immature stage for as many as five or six years. Like many desert animals, the bees avoid the heat of day for work. The average life of the adult bee is about six weeks. *Dianthidium, Anthidiellum, Anthidium, Perdita, Colletes,* and *Ashmediella* are common genera of arid regions.

The cuckoo bees (*Nomadidae*), often with bodies of a bright metallic blue or green with yellow markings, live as guests in the nests of other bees. Cuckoolike, the female lays her eggs in the nectar- and pollen-provisioned nests of other bees. If, as often happens, her eggs hatch first and her larvae feed more rapidly than those of the host larvae, the latter may die of starvation.

Those insects of plastic behavior, the ants, are well adapted to arid lands, since many of them get on perfectly well without recourse to drinking. They generally find sources of water and food in the seeds and insect larvae which seasonally appear. The most widespread and abundant ants are naturally the seed-eating or harvester ants, for it is these that have the most dependable sources of food.

The large craterlike nests of the black harvester ant (*Messor pergandei*) are found in great abundance, particularly on the Mohave Desert north of the Santa Fe Railway. No matter how stony the soil, they are certain to appear; even the bleak stretches of desert pavement are nesting sites for them if saltbushes are near at hand to furnish seeds. The small ants are shiny black, and all day long you may see the tiny workmen busily engaged in bringing up little stones from the underground tunnels or gathering seeds to store in their granaries. The seeds are taken below and hulled, and the rejected chaff is brought up and placed upon the outer edge of the craterlike nest.

Another harvester (*Messor andrei*) is also common. The nests of this ant are built on smooth ground and the craters consist mostly of the chaff of wild buckwheat and alfilaree. The thorax is brownish, but the other parts are shiny black.

Then there are the large and powerful harvesters belonging to the genus *Pogonomyrmex*. The bearded harvester (*P. barbatus*) has a black head and thorax, but the gaster (abdomen) is reddish. It, like many other desert ants, must frequently remove the accumulation of dust and sand from its body. Special combs on its forelegs are used for this purpose. These combs are in turn cleaned by passing them through curious, basketlike "beards" of long hairs on the under surface of the head. Radiating from the large gravel craters which reveal the location of the nests, long lines of workers may be seen going to and returning from the forage fields. Sometimes the lines are a handsbreadth in width and two hundred yards long. The ants work only during the day but in midsummer they are out by 4:00 A.M. Wide clearings, two to twelve feet in diameter, are made about the nest openings and even the paths are kept free from vegetation. When rains come, circles of grass often spring up from seeds left about the refuse heaps.

The occidental harvester (*P. occidentalis*) is a large, reddish ant building conspicuous mounds of pebbles. These mounds are from four to twelve inches high and from two to three feet in diameter, and have small, cleared spaces about them. The entrance to the underground repositories is usually near the base of the mound. The passageways are closed at night, and several guards remain on duty at the opening. This ant has two spinelike projections on the last portion of the thorax.

The remarkable honey-pot ants (*Myrmecocystus mexicanus*), which turn certain of their numbers into veritable living bottles of honey, may be recognized by their light amber-colored bodies. The nests are usually made in sandy places, but gravelly soils may also be chosen. I remember once coming upon a nest in the early morning, and, thinking it was a small colony because there were but three watchmen about the entrance, I ventured to open it. Before beginning excavations, I tapped the ground vigorously, and a great swarm of soldiers rushed out with amazing suddenness and began moving about with those excited strides so characteristic of the group. Inside I found the galleries fairly teeming with workers and numbers of repletes, as the ants which serve as living honey reservoirs are called. These honey ants are highly insectivorous.

Of unusual interest are the locally found parasol ants (belonging to the group *Attini*) which occur on the warmer parts of the Colorado Desert. They are given to cutting off leaves, usually of leguminious trees, and carrying them like sunshades over their backs. These they store in deep and extensive subterranean chambers. We sometimes see the leaf-transporting ants in long lines crossing the sandy washes. On the stored leaves are grown ambrosia fungi as food for themselves and their larvae. The fungi are cultivated in special chambers where they are tended by workers which eliminate all but pure cultures. The nests can be located not only by following the ants but by the turret-shaped craters, about the entrances of which are often seen bright yellow fungus masses which have been discarded.

Those furry-backed insects which so energetically wander about on the sands, and which are known as fuzzy ants or cow killers, are really solitary, parasitic wasps. Only the males bear wings. The largest one known from the California deserts is the satanic mutillid (*Dasymutilla satanus*), a rather robust insect whose back is adorned with a deep pile of reddish-orange hair. Mention must also be made of the sand wanderer (*D. arenivaga*), a medium-sized, less showy species, having the body covered with hoary and yellow hairs. The small mutillid, known as the "little old man of the sands" (*D. gloriosa*), stands in strong contrast to its more colorful relatives in having its body black and its legs sparsely covered with long white hairs.

The great majority of the butterflies seen on our deserts,

such as the anise swallowtail and the alfalfa yellow, are also
common near the coast. It is of interest to note that the chalcedon checkerspot, which in the coastal district shows black as
its dominant color, is found locally on the desert with red
predominating. Of the butterflies found only on the desert,
the great yellow, two-tailed papilio (*Papilio multicaudata*),
confined to the northern Mohave, is the largest. A number of
white-winged butterflies are not infrequently seen flying together. Becker's pierid (*Pieris beckeri*), whose larvae feed on
bladder pod, is found on both deserts, but the other three
whites are exclusively Mohavean species whose larvae feed
on mustards. The southern marble (*Euchloe creusa lotta*),
known by the remarkable green color on the underside of the
secondary wings, the rare desert orangetip (*Anthecharis
ceuthura*), and the California white (*Pieris sisymbrii*) are all
early fliers and may be taken in late March and early April.

The larvae of the little desert dwarf, the chara checkerspot
(*Melitea chara*), feeds on the beloperone and nothing else; it
is therefore confined wholly to the Colorado Desert. It is the
smallest of all the California checkerspots and is difficult to
see unless the insects are flying in great numbers. The eggs of
Neumoegen's checkerspot (*Melitea neumoegenii*), a Mohavean species, are laid in a single mass at the foot of the flower
stems of the Mohave aster (*Aster abatus*). The young caterpillars start feeding on the dainty stamens of the flowers, but
as they get stronger they feed on the petals and finally on the
leaves.

The rufescent patch (*Chlosyne lacinia crocale*) is a striking
black butterfly, local in California on the Colorado Desert,
but widely distributed in Arizona, Texas, and New Mexico.
The normal food plant is the sunflower. The dainty, juniper-
feeding thecla (*Metoura siva juniperiana*), with bronzy-
brown upper-wings and underparts of green, brown, and
white, flies from mid-March to mid-April. Since it seldom
leaves its food plant, you must beat the bushes to get it. It

may fly up in the air, but you are certain to see it soon settling again.

The San Emigdio blue butterfly (*Plebjus emigdionis*) shows a remarkable purple sheen on its small, blue wings. It is a saltbush feeder and the underside of the wings, which shows when the insect is at rest, exactly matches the gray color of the food plant. The small blue butterfly (*Philotes speciosa*) lays its eggs on *Oxytheca perfoliata,* and when they hatch the tiny larvae begin to devour the green food in the center of the spine-tipped bracts. After feeding is over, it curls around the stem and rests, appearing now for all the world like a little seed in the bottom of the stem-pierced cup. As the mature insects try to fly in the strong winds that prevail in the spring on the Mohave Desert they stay close to the ground. When they alight to rest they seek a sunny place on the sand. Then, hooking the three legs of one side to a pebble, they allow the wind to blow them over parallel to the ground, the position of least resistance. How very clever!

It is the small moths that excel in number of species. Let the traveler begin to collect the myriads of kinds that hover about and dash into his campfire or the glare of his auto light, and he will be amazed at their number and beauty. There is not a month of the year when the collector's ardor will not be rewarded. The pupal life of many of them is spent out of sight underground, but a few are conspicuous because of the peculiar pupal cases they hang on desert plants. The larva of the creosote psyche or bag worm builds a silken, cigar-shaped case ornamented with the tips of creosote leaves. This is carried about as the larva feeds. In this case it also pupates, and it is common to find the brown cocoons hung among the branches of the creosote bushes. Remarkably, the female, which develops in the case, never leaves the silken tube, even being fertilized there and laying her eggs within it. The larvae of the chilopsis moth (*Eucaterva variaria*) feed on the leaves of the desert willow and build meshed cocoons of tan-colored silk through which the pupae may be seen. These cases, which are hung high on the branches of the trees, appear like "wads of crumpled gauze," each about the size of a large olive.

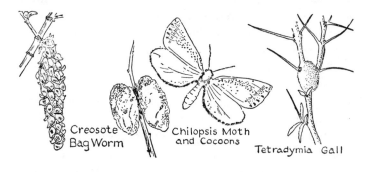

Creosote Bag Worm

Chilopsis Moth and Cocoons

Tetradymia Gall

Among insects coming into the desert recently must be mentioned the giant riparian earwig (*Labidura riparia*). It is predatory on caterpillars. Housewives do not like it because of its bad smell. This nonflying insect has been distributed all over the world by man. It came into California about 1955.

OTHER INVERTEBRATES

In lifting up old boards or stones you are certain at some time or other to spy one of the yellow- or green-brown scorpions. If the weather is warm this strange-appearing creature of the wild will probably almost immediately begin to move away with its crablike claws menacingly upraised and its long sting-terminated "tail" curled over its back. Chances are very good it is one of the kind that holds no particular danger to man, although its sting may be lethal to those small creatures (insects, spiders, centipedes, etc.) which normally are its prey. In southern Arizona and northeastern Mexico there are small scorpions *(Centruroides)* whose sting may inject a poison that may be lethal to a child, but so far as I can learn they do not occur in California. Scorpions are very greedy feeders and seem most of the time to be very hungry; if necessary, however, they may go for long periods without food. They produce living young and these ride on the mother's back, taking no food until after the first molt, when they begin to fend for themselves. A layer of wax in the hard body covering protects scorpions from excessive loss of water. To control body temperature somewhat, they may straighten the legs in such a way as to raise the body off the hot earth. They can do without water for a long time. On the underside of the body is a unique pair of comblike organs, pectines of uncertain function, though they probably serve as tactile organs, especially during the mating period.

The pseudo-scorpions are small brown creatures, scarcely more than an eighth of an inch long, which appear for all the world like tiny tailless scorpions. The abdomen is rounded behind. These are alert creatures, wholly harmless, that feed upon mites and young insects too weak to defend themselves. They can run swiftly, often in a jerky manner, backward as well as forward and sidewise. By attaching themselves to the bodies of such insects as flies and beetles they are transported from place to place. When moulting, silk is spun to make an enclosure for protection. Sensory hairs of the body and pedipalpi take the place of eyes in apprising them of their surroundings.

Spiders, like ants, are more or less common wherever one goes. Only those of more specialized habits can contend successfully, however, with the rapid fluctuations in the abundance of insects on which they live.

Among the numerous species of desert spiders there are several that are widespread and also very noticeable because of their unique webs or their size. Spiders of the genus *Diguetia* (named after M. Diguet, an amateur collector) make rather ragged-looking gray silken tubes about two inches long which they hang by irregular webs in shrubs. The opening is at the bottom of the hollow case and the small spider lurks within.

Sometimes the sides as well as the orifice of this hideout are decorated with pieces of small insects, the trophies of her chase, and small bits of plant stems. *Diguetia canites* has been noted in the Chuckawalla Mountains, *D. mohavea* from Yermo, and *D. signata* from Palm Desert.

Gray hairy lycosid or wolf spiders of rather large size (an inch to an inch and a half overall spread) dig tubular holes, often in hard soils, sometimes a foot or more deep with a side tunnel in which they rest. They usually ring the burrow opening with a conspicuous collar of soil particles and fragments of the stems of plants bound together with silk. They are extremely shy creatures and must be dug from their burrows if we wish to see them. They do their hunting at night, probably not going far from their retreat.

Many people associate the big brown or near-black hairy tarantulas only with deserts, but they are also abundant in many less arid environments. They, too, make deep vertical tunnels. Most of those seen slowly wandering about in the daytime are males looking for mates. The males are often short-lived but the females may attain a considerable age. It takes about ten years for the female to mature. In spite of their frightening appearance, tarantulas are harmless creatures and should never be killed.

There is a rather small, light-colored labyrinth spider *(Metepeira gosona)* that often appears in great numbers in autumn. It usually selects, it seems by preference, the creosote bush for the site of the strong, orb web which it stretches in generous style among the branches. Somewhere near the center of the orb is hung a conspicuous, ragged, cylindrical retreat, made of silk and perhaps decorated with bits of dried leaves and sticks. It is about an inch long, of the diameter of a pencil, and is the spider's daytime abode. In it the lens-shaped egg-cases are hung.

In late September in almost every creosote bush of certain districts of the Mohave Desert can be found a cylindrical, silken retreat about the size of the last joint of the little finger. It is unaccompanied by a web and is the home of a handsome jumping spider, *Phidippus nikites.* This is a large, heavily built spider about half an inch long, for the most part black and with deep vermilion or salmon marks on the back of the abdomen and cephalo-thorax. The male runs about freely on the branches, but the female, which builds the retreat in which to hide the egg-case, is usually confined to a position near her silken domicile. The dainty-stemmed buckwheats, found in summer in such abundance about the borders of dry-type playas, are most excellent places to look for spiders of many species. One little spider (*Singa* sp.?) hangs her white, lentil-shaped egg-case in the forks of the stems and hides underneath it until the young emerge. These egg-sacs are often so plentiful that the plants holding them appear to be white with flowers.

Crab-spiders, belonging to the family *Thomisidae,* are fond of lurking in flowers. These spiders have the habit of moving with facility sidewise and backward as well as forward. A particularly interesting one is a flower-haunting species living in the flowers of the evening primrose (*Oenothera deltoides*), of the sand dunes. In her white and yellow garb, she lies in wait for honey-eating insects. The question is where she is and what she is doing during the long summer drought after all the primroses have dried to crispness.

To the lycosid spiders must be ascribed the curious little chimneys of sticks and silk which surmount the tops of the deep, tubular holes we so often see on the flat stretches of sand and clay. The taciturn, brown-bodied occupants spend their days at the bottoms of their burrows, venturing forth only at night for their insect prey.

The small angellito or red velvet mite (*Dinothrombidium pandorae*) of the Coachella Valley suddenly appears in almost unbelievable numbers on areas of fine sands after midwinter rains of a quarter-inch or more. The handsome creatures emerge from their burrows on the first sunny morning after an adequate rain and feed on subterranean termites also brought out by the moisture. The reproduction period is a brief hour or so. If the day continues sunny they soon re-enter the sand, digging new vertical burrows four and a half to six inches deep to hide in. The plugs of loose, moist sand forced to the surface as they dig form little mounds, which if in great numbers are fairly conspicuous on the dune surfaces. Once buried, the mites remain submerged throughout the summer. Winter brings on a short period of cold-induced dormancy. As soon as the days begin to warm and rain ensues they are ready to come forth again. Eggs are laid in the burrows. The embryos develop eyes and legs in about a month and the larvae appear soon after. Then they crawl to the surface and search for grasshoppers, upon which they live for a short period as parasites. After awhile they drop off their hosts and enter the sand, there to complete the development to maturity.

Although in many places the amount of moisture and humus in the soil is almost imperceptible, there is frequently enough to make life possible for millipedes, those queer, brown, cylindrical, many-legged near-relatives of the centipedes. There are quite a number of strictly desert species found in the low desert mountains and intervening valleys. They not only tunnel beneath stones or go into the crevices of rocks but also go down the burrows of rodents or of insects or into excavations of their own digging. After rains, particularly at night, millipedes come forth to breed and to feed on decaying vegetation. Their presence on deserts is taken as an additional argument for the belief in a more humid past.

The voracious buff-brown solpugids or sun spiders are most commonly seen only at night. They are swift movers that run almost constantly about on the ground seeking their prey, mainly insects, large and small, spiders, and young scorpions. These they greedily grasp between the four forward-directed jaws which they move up and down, thus effectively cutting up their victims. These hairy creatures are sometimes called vinegaroons, a name properly reserved for the whip-scorpions which actually do at times emit a vinegarlike odor. The many hairs covering the long legs are properly called setae. In some species they are very long and exceedingly sensitive to the lightest contact, provoking an immediate response. There are no poison glands, hence these arachnids need not be feared. They may make burrows to hide in or they may seek shelter under stones or in crevices, perhaps even under your sleeping bag.

Especially after heavy summer rains there may appear in unbelievable numbers in the rock pools of the canyons and in other ponded waters, dainty, almost transparent, fairy, clam, or tadpole shrimps. The eggs, which have long lain quiescent in the dust, perhaps over a period of years, suddenly hatch in the warm water. Development is very rapid—in fact, the whole life history of these graceful swimming creatures may have a span of only fifteen days. Food evidently consists of suddenly exploding populations of microscopic protozoans, diatoms, and primitive algae. Sometimes a species is abundant for several successive summers, then the next year is unaccountably absent. The drought-resistant resting eggs constitute nature's sole device for tiding over populations from one favorable season to another, perhaps over a period of twelve to fifteen years. They are distributed by wind, perhaps on the feet of water birds which sometimes light on the surface of the pools and feed on these eucrustaceans.

In the spring season, particularly at night, which is their time for roving, the soft, spherical-bodied granddaddy long-legs or harvestmen are busy scampering among the rocks or herbage. They are said to be very thirsty animals and to depend not alone on the colorless blood of their victims (the young of insects, spiders, and mites) for moisture but also upon water from dewdrops or succulent plants. Under these conditions they must necessarily be conspiciously scarce in the summer season. The desert species are probably short-lived, their day being co-terminous with the moist season. The eggs (twenty to forty) are placed, without protection of cocoons, in cracks of the soil or under rocks or bark. It is rather difficult to find an animal that has not lost a leg or two. Lost limbs cannot be regenerated.

The rocky and often barren-looking hills and mountains of the desert would hardly seem the places to look for snails, but they are there and the species are many. Even the very dry-appearing ranges of the Death Valley region have them. Almost all the granitic ranges harbor them. The empty and often beautifully brown-banded porcelainlike shells show up along the margins of dry, sandy streamways or shallow rock crevices where they have been left by the freshets following heavy rains. During most of the year the living animals lie hidden deep in the earth beneath rocks or in rock crevices, in a state of quiescence. But let the rains come and they are soon out of hiding, especially at night, searching for succulent plants on which they feed with aid of the toothed rasping organ called the radula. Sometimes we see them crawling about in the early morning hours, especially if the sky is overcast. When the days get warm and dry they secrete a mucouslike substance and seal up the orifice of their shells with a tough papery membrane called an epiphragm, thus avoiding desiccation. Often they are sealed tight against a rock. Sometimes in order to avoid extremes of dryness and heat they bury themselves three or four feet beneath the earth's surface, perhaps in a rock slide.

Several genera of land snails are present. Snails of the genus *Micrarionta* are most widespread, especially on the Mohave Desert. Along the western rim of the Colorado Desert snails, somewhat larger ones, representing the genus *Helmintho-glypta* are found. In the higher limestone ranges of the eastern Mohave Desert (especially Clark Mountain) the genus *Oreohelix* is represented.

Most all those small shells you may pick up on the sands of the Salton Basin are modern. They are remains of a freshwater fauna left stranded as the waters of former fresh to brackish water lakes receded and finally dried up. Here and there they may be so plentiful after winds have exposed them that the sands are white with them. Among the lot are the shells of a clam (*Anodonta californiensis*) and of small snails such as *Physa humerosa, Hydrobia protea, Helisoma traskii, Pelidostrema longigua,* and *Pyrgulopsis* of three species. A few fossil marine mollusks are sometimes found but they are rare.

In 1937 Allyn G. Smith of Berkeley discovered in the highly mineralized water at Badwater in Death Valley, a minute thin-shelled snail (*Asiminea infirma*). It lives among the crevices of crystalline salt, and also among roots of the salt-loving plant called allenrolfia, and has the distinction of being the only soft-bodied invertebrate to inhabit a saturated salt solution. A number of small fresh-water snails may be collected at Saratoga Springs and other fresh-water pools in Death Valley. Fossil mollusks of a number of kinds, among them ammonites, are known to occur in the Valley's rocks of marine origin.

Nematodes or threadworms, living either as parasites or commensals, are represented by many species. They are partial to soil zones below the dry six-inch mantle and there they associate mainly with the roots of plants. Many of these are harmless to their associated hosts; they may even be beneficial, for they reduce the small amounts of underground humus to a form that can be utilized by the plants.

6. Fishes, Frogs, and Toads

Even the arid regions of the earth are not without their fishes. In the sunny waters of some of the tepid or hot springs (72° to 93° F.) of the Mohave Desert, in and near Death Valley, swim bluish-brown minnows of the genus *Cyprinodon*. The finding of fish in these isolated springs was a great surprise to the early travelers, and the uninformed of today still raise the question how they got there. In reply it must be said that these fish, now found in segregated waters, are probably relicts from an ancient stream system which in Pleistocene times, or later, connected these springs.

Recent studies show that, although minor differences have developed during their long isolation, these fish probably came originally from common ancestors. Excepting one fish population from Ash Meadows, Nevada, all are considered to belong to the species *macularius*. Similar if not identical minnows are found in warm alkaline springs of the Salton Basin (Fish Springs, Dos Palmos). The Ash Meadow minnow, because of its dark color and small size and the shape of the teeth, has been described as a new species (*C. diabolis*). In the different populations the characters vary with the temperature, the fish in hotter waters exhibiting the greatest differences. It is of interest to note that fish of this genus, *Cy-*

prinodon, live also in briny springs and hot pools of the Sahara and Dead Sea deserts. Like those living in our desert pools, some have suffered the modification or loss of their ventral fins.

When we turn to the consideration of the native fish of the Mohave River we find further evidence that the ancient streams of the Mohave Desert were integrated into a single river system, with Death Valley Lake acting as the important link that connected them. Two fishes now inhabit the Mohave River, the common introduced catfish (*Amiurus nebulosus*) and a native minnow (*Siphateles mohavensis*), the last closely related to a minnow of the Owens River (*S. obesus*). "It seems quite likely," says David Thompson, "that an ancestral form of *Siphateles obesus* which now inhabits Owens River may have traveled through the Owens–Death Valley system and through a permanent or temporary lake in Death Valley and entered the Mohave River basin where it became modified to the *S. mohavensis* form."

The first fish to swim in the briny waters of the Salton Sea came in, for the most part, with the incursion of the Colorado River in 1905–6. At one time they existed in quantities sufficient to tempt Portuguese fishermen to make a commercial venture of them. Among fish now known to live there are the hump-backed sucker, the Mullet, and the Colorado River trout. Carp, once so abundant, have largely disappeared. The small desert cyprinodont and another minnow (*Gambusia affinis*) are common along the shallow shore waters.

Our desert's toad and frog fauna is a limited one. Except for the species inhabiting the Colorado River and connecting streams, the explanation of their interrupted and limited distribution is found in remembering that in those more humid days that prevailed in the geologic past there were means of dispersion which, to animals so wedded to water as the frogs and toads, are no longer available.

The red-spotted toad (*Bufo punctatus*) is a species confined wholly to the deserts of the southwestern United States
and northern Mexico. It is found in canyons where permanent seepage and springs occur. The best field-marks other
than its diminutive size (it is less than three inches long) are
the small, squat, vermilion-tipped warts that appear like
handsome jewels on its back. Spawning takes place in April
and the toads may then be heard in loud song, adding new
melodious notes to the chorus of spring. The cricketlike voice
is long-continued and shrill. The little gray throat swells out
into a rounded pouchlike sack; "just like he had swallowed a
marble," said an old prospector. These toads are for the most
part nocturnal, hiding during the day in rock crevices on the
borders of the streams and spring basins. During dry periods
they may hide under rocks where the air is somewhat humid.
If the soil is damp, water may be absorbed through the "seat-
patch." "The toad *Bufo punctatus*," says Dr. Rodolfo Riubal, "can store as much as 30 per cent of its gross body weight
as water in the urinary bladder. This bladder urine is the
principal water reservoir of the animal. Under conditions of
dehydration the bladder water is resorbed and permits the
toad to exert a degree of homeostatic control of the concentration of the blood and lymph. As dehydration progresses
the concentration of the urine rises and presumably when
the urine is isotonic [having equal osmotic pressure] to the
lymph (or blood) the concentration of lymph also starts to
rise. Toads dehydrated after the bladder has been emptied
of water demonstrate no water reserve."

A small population of the leopard frog (*Rana pipiens*),
which has the widest range of any North American am-
phibian, has recently been found in the brackish water of
San Felipe Creek near where it empties into the Salton Sea.

Couch's spadefoot toad (*Scaphiopus couchi*) commonly
breeds in temporary rain pools in the Lower Sonoran deserts.
It is called a spadefoot toad because of the tubercle or "spade"

on the hind foot which it uses in digging in the sand to bury itself to escape the heat and to prevent desiccation. On our Colorado Desert it is very limited in distribution, being found only in areas east of the lower end of the Salton Sea and in the vicinity of the Algodones Dunes. There it is particularly evident as it comes from hiding and lays its eggs in temporary pools following summer cloudbursts. Almost immediately after egg-laying it buries itself.

The very large Colorado River toad (*Bufo alvarius*) occurs not only along the lower Colorado River but also eastward in arid portions of Arizona, principally in the drainage of the Gila River. It is most evident after summer rains but it is also seen sparingly at other times. It has a skin secretion which is particularly toxic to dogs and may prove fatal if the dog takes the toad in its mouth. The loud voice is said to suggest "a ferryboat whistle" when heard alone, but all too often it is eclipsed by the chorus of quacks and lamentations from the spadefoot and other toads inhabiting the same areas.

The Pacific tree toad (*Hyla regilla*) is a hardy little creature of greenish hue, scarcely more than two inches long. The best field-marks for the use of the novice are the adhesive pads on the fingers and toes and the dark stripe along the side of the head. This toad is widely distributed on the Pacific Coast and in many points of the desert, except in the extreme southeastern portion. The cry of the males, "Kreck-rk," uttered over and over again in rapid succession, is always good evidence of the full approach of spring. The adults hide, not in trees as the name would imply, but in rock crevices and under vegetation about the springs. In the evening they shamble forth on the banks, intent upon snapping up insects.

The drab livery of the sand-colored tree toad (*Hyla californiae = arenicolor*) is an adaptation apparently physiological. It is always some tone of gray with close resemblance to the granite boulders among the crevices in which the animal rests. This is its means of defying detection, for it appears, indeed, quite like a mere "bump on a rock." The species is one from desert canyons carrying perennial streams, and there one often hears the quacking music of the male, especially in spring. The notes are made with the mouth held wide open. The animals spend most of their time, not in water, but on rock surfaces where they flatten out, often several or many together. They keep the body temperature down through evaporation of water from the skin.

7. Reptile Life

Lizards are perhaps the most conspicuous and the most frequently seen larger animals of our deserts. Summer travelers are particularly interested in them because of the numbers they see on the pavements of the desert roads. and they are not less surprised at the speed that some of them show when frightened by the approach of an automobile.

Appearing for all the world like some small, slender-bodied, gray-white mammal, the crested keel-backed lizard or iguana (*Dipsosaurus dorsalis*) dashes wildly across the glaring sands, stopping only when he considers himself far beyond reach. Then, turning around, he raises himself high on stilted limbs and gazes as his pursuer, ready at a moment's notice to continue his flight to some other position of safety. On the southern deserts individuals are out as early as late March. They then may be seen in pairs playing about or basking in the sun on old prostrate ironwood logs or on sand hummocks. On the Mohave Desert they do not come from their winter retreats in the sand until fully a month later. The usual color is tawny brown or grayish, with darker bars and spots running both longitudinally and transversely. When they are angered, reddish-brown circles appear on their backs. One taken on the dunes of the Amargosa Desert of Nevada measured more than two feet in length, fully half of which was tail. Since it was in winter, when food was scarce, the lizard's leathery skin hung shaggily over its gaunt frame. This grotesque lizard is unique in having a dorsal crest or comb of strongly keeled scales, beginning just at the back of the head and running almost the length of the tail. As the animal raises itself on its limbs to run, the scales are erected, giving it a most formidable appearance. It lives about the dunes and sandy washes, frequently seeking protection in burrows under shrubs and mesquite trees. Like the chuckawalla, the keel-backed lizard is able to inflate its body in order to prevent its enemies from extracting it from the crevices or holes in which it has sought safety. During the heat of the day we may find it feeding on flowers of the creosote bush or on the leaves of such small shrubs and trees as it can climb. It is said to be the most heat-tolerant of any of our desert lizards. If the sun gets too warm it may go underground into its "home burrow" or into the tunnel of some small mammal. It may be forced to go underground by extreme desiccation. In winter it hibernates.

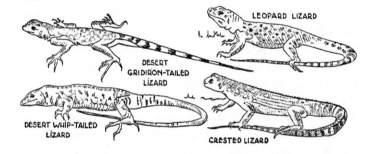

Lizards, like snakes, are cold-blooded animals, but this does not mean that they have no control of their internal body temperature. They regulate their body heat both by exposing themselves in favorable positions to the sun, particularly in the early morning hours, and by retreating into shade or descending into cool burrows if unduly warm.

At that time of late spring when the sands are dazzling under the white rays of the desert sun and the ephemeral flowers are giving way under a wilting dryness, the gridiron- or zebra-tailed lizard (*Callisaurus draconoides*) is making itself evident in almost every gravelly waste. It is the season of mating, and even the murderous callisaurus is feeling the impulse of love. Again and again I have seen pairs of them going through the fancy curves of the courting dance, waltzing back and forth in curious frolics like a pair of amorous mockingbirds. The movements, full of grace and curious rhythm, are engaged in for long periods. On such occasions gridiron-tailed lizards may be approached with ease, but on all others they are excessively wild. While hunting, the slender body is carried close to the ground with the tail curled up at the end; but let an individual be alarmed and it raises itself and runs away with full enjoyment of its vigorous powers of flight and at incredible speed. When finally it stops, the animal turns around and steadily gazes at its pursuer in a wild, resentful manner, with head and shoulders raised high and limbs held ready to speed on at a moment's notice. If hard pressed, it dives out of sight in the sand or retreats into rodent holes with a cleverness that must outwit the most wily pursuer. The gridiron-tailed lizard is a greedy feeder and often snaps up the smaller lizards as its legitimate prey, swallowing the recalcitrant victims alive. Other food consists of insects and the buds and green leaves of the desert herbs. The black bands which adorn the tail vary in number from four to eight and are always a conspicuous means of identification. The body takes on the whitish color of the silver sands so that it is often impossible to see the lizard until it starts on its mad dash to safety. Two brilliant, bluish-black bars ornament the sides of the body of the males.

Another successful candidate for notoriety as a runner is

the desert whiptailed lizard (*Cnemidophorus tigris*). A momentary glimpse is all we may obtain of the swift-moving form as it skims over the sands on a burning midsummer day. It seems to maintain itself in a perpetual state of alertness and generally eludes us even on our most vigilant chases. Confident of its strength, and as if playing some sort of game, it keeps just far enough ahead to be out of reach. The stalker of this wary lizard must manifest the greatest self-control. In order to frustrate his designs, it often dives into the shelter of a bush, where it may mask its presence among the shadows of the branches. These swift-jacks, as they are sometimes called because of their rapidity of movement, have, while hunting, the curious habit of creeping jerkily over the sands, at the same time thrusting out their tongues. I recently saw one behaving after this manner and was surprised to find it later using its forefeet for digging, a habit common enough among mammals but rather unusual among lizards. A single foot was brought into play, while it kept watch for the object of its search—a small, burrowing insect.

The leopard lizard (*Crotaphytus wislisenii*) is, like its gridiron-tailed cousin, a denizen of the broad stretches of the sandy mesas and washes of the open desert. In spite of its large body it is capable of great speed and if caught in disadvantageous positions is able to give its pursuer a merry and prolonged chase before being taken. The hotter the day the more interesting and racy the pursuit. When undisturbed, this lizard spends much time skulking about in the flecking shadows of the low desert shrubs around and upon which it finds much of its food. The silver-winged grasshopper, singing in the creosote bushes, is often snatched from its perch by a leaping crotaphytus, which may have jumped three times its own length to get it. In Pinto Basin in Riverside County I caught a large male swallowing a crested lizard almost his own size. Strange to say, the two-thirds-devoured saurian, though wounded about the head, soon recovered when spewed from the mouth of his cannibalistic cousin and before long seemed as lively as ever. The diet of the leopard lizard is varied by eating blossoms and leaves of herbaceous annuals.

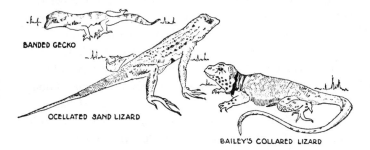

BANDED GECKO

OCELLATED SAND LIZARD

BAILEY'S COLLARED LIZARD

The ocellated sand lizards of the genus *Uma,* with peculiar blotched markings, are limited to the sandy wastes and shifting, wind-blown sand of dunes such as occur along the Mohave River, on the Mohave Desert, and on territory contiguous to the Colorado River. You are certain to see them on the Algodones Dunes near Yuma. They are wary, swift runners, and they have the remarkable habit of burying themselves beneath the sand when pursued, leaving only a puff of dust as evidence of their place of retreat. When flushed from hiding, a sand lizard makes a rapid dash across the open, to secrete itself again. A curious adaptation to its habitat is seen in the fringes of elongate scales which broaden the toes and increase its ability to burrow and also to run rapidly over the loose sands. Its food consists of insects—ants, beetles, bees, grasshoppers—and the leaves of herbaceous annuals. Because of its narrow range of heat tolerance, uma's sand-surface activities are limited to a small portion of daylight hours.

The Coachella sand lizard (*Uma inornata*) is confined to an area northwest of Indio; the Colorado Desert sand lizard (*Uma notata*) lives in loose wind-blown sands of the area south, west, and east of the Salton Sea, thence over into nearby Arizona and Sonora (Punta Peñasco). *Uma scoparia,* the Mohave sand lizard, is wholly a Mohavean species.

The chuckawalla (*Sauromalus obesus*) is California's largest native lizard and most bizarre in form. A full-grown individual may reach a length of eighteen inches and have a body four inches wide. This is a rock-loving species, seldom found in open sandy spaces. When the sun is blazing hot, chuckawallas become most lively; however, their thermal tolerance is not exceedingly high. In winter they hibernate. Though their bodies are of obese proportions, they are clever at dodging and when pressed by a pursuer they may run at considerable speed. The chase is generally ended when the lizard darts into a deep rock crevice and inflates its body so greatly that it is impossible to extract it. When caught in open places, chuckawallas defend themselves by long, lashing strokes of the tail, or they may resort to biting. I am well aware through experience that the teeth of a full-grown adult are capable of inflicting painful wounds.

The chuckawalla is a thoroughgoing vegetarian but may occasionally eat insect larvae. During the days of spring it is a greedy feeder on flowers and it even climbs into small shrubs to get them. Several times I have seen one high up among the fat stems of the brittlebush, snapping with heavy jaws at the yellow blossoms. When flowers are not available, both leaves and green stems are eaten. Even such bitter, aromatic shrubs as the burroweed and the creosote bush are not shunned.

During winter and also at night, retreats are sought in deep rock crevices. When spring opens, chuckawallas come forth lean and gaunt and are often too weak to run. Under such conditions they are easily snapped up by birds of prey, which doubtless prize them as food for nestling young.

The body color and pattern vary considerably in different individuals, especially in the young. The finely beaded skin is often grayish-brown, dark-brown, or black, with markings of red-brown. The fat, scaly tail is often white or light gray and girdled by broad black bands.

Sooner or later, when turning over stones, you will come upon the gentle banded gecko (*Coleonyx variegatus*), a little lizard of handsome color and pleasing manner. The loose skin has an almost waxy appearance, while the upper surface varies in color from yellowish to fawn, relieved by the beautiful walnut-brown transverse bands of the back and tail. The peculiar, small, fleshy spurs on the sides of the tail near its root are certain to arouse our interest. A full-grown adult measures about four inches in length. The curious habit of emitting a feeble, squeaking noise when disturbed is always a delightful surprise to the listener. Often the timid creature opens its mouth as if yawning, then proceeds to lick its jaws, like a little dog that has just finished a meal. When it desires to move it raises itself on its weak limbs with the aid of its tail, presenting a picture of helplessness which almost arouses in one an emotion of compassion.

The beautiful Mearns's uta (*Uta mearnsi*) is confined largely to the west side of the Colorado Desert, where it frequents the boulders and vertical rock walls of the deep mountain gorges. In the low mountains west of Brawley, it is the commonest lizard seen. It is sometimes confused with Bailey's collared lizard because of the presence of the narrow band of intense black between its shoulders. When, however, the two lizards are compared, the difference at once becomes obvious: Mearns's uta has a single, black shoulder-band, whereas Bailey's lizard has two. It is extraordinarily shy and when approached quickly runs beyond reach or hastens to conceal itself. When caught, it attempts to defend itself by biting. Hunting goes on all through the day, but there is less activity when the heat becomes intense. So clever are the maneuvers in stalking the insect prey that I have passed away many a pleasant hour watching them boldly leaping from rock to rock or creeping along granite surfaces to get into positions most advantageous for capturing the insects they were stalking. The vision must be keen, for I have seen them commence their stalking movements when more than five feet from a fly.

The desert brown-shouldered lizard (*Uta stansburiana elegans*) is such a lively little creature and such a frequent visitor to the environs of our desert camps that we cannot but feel it is our choice from among all our saurian neighbors. Acting the host, we are inclined to invite it to our premises and give it permission to catch all the flies it can get without fear of molestation. Of all its peculiar antics there is none more engaging that that of spasmodically bobbing the body as it nervously fidgets about while stalking its winged insect-prey. In the breeding season the metallic-blue spots on its sides are very conspicuous and give an added charm to the mottled, brownish-gray coat of this little saurian aristocrat of the desert rocks.

The small, long-tailed brush lizard (*Urosaurus graciosus*), conspicuous because of its extraordinarily long tail, is a denizen of the sands and brushy areas such as those bordering the Colorado River and in the Coachella Valley. "Long-tailed utas like to sun themselves," says Dr. Camp, "on the topmost twig of a bush, hanging motionless and head downwards as though pinned there by a shrike. If disturbed they drop to the middle of the bush and flatten themselves against a limb lengthwise, keeping on the side away from the intruder, their wiry tails stretched out stiffly in line with the body. When alarmed while on the ground they make for the nearest bush and jump into it, there to dodge actively about among the branches, quite unlike their brown-shouldered relatives, which usually retreat beneath stones or into holes when pursued."

In California the beautifully marked Arizona tree uta (*Uta ornata symmetrica*) occurs only among the wooded bottoms of the Colorado River between Yuma and Needles, but in Arizona it is widely distributed from the Grand Canyon to the southern borders of the state. It may be distinguished from the desert brown-shouldered lizard, which to the uninitiated it in many ways resembles, by the presence of the longitudinal dorso-lateral skin-fold and by the absence of the rounded, blue blotch behind the axilla. It spends much of its time climbing over the bark of the willows and other river-bottom trees, seeking insects.

Those who are curious to see the vigilant desert night lizard (*Xantusia vigilis*) will usually find it hiding in holes and crevices or under bark of decaying yucca stems. When first brought out into the light it seems dazed but soon shows signs of life and attempts by means of its diminutive legs to get away to a place of hiding. The smoky-gray color of the body blends perfectly with the peculiar setting in which nature intended it to be seen. If handled at all roughly, the small, timid creature generally drops the tail, leaving it to squirm out of the hand and slither over the ground. Termites, ants, spiders, ticks, caterpillars and springtails, which probably constitute its principal food, are mostly hunted at night but also sometimes by day. This small lizard usually gives birth to two young.

The desert scaly lizard (*Sceloporus magister*), sometimes called the desert spiny lizard, is a rather large, heavily built saurian with prominent scales over most of its body. Its spiny armor adapts it to move with ease among the bushes where it resides. Individuals are often seen climbing about wood-rats' nests, in cactus bushes, and in mesquite trees. Theirs is a mixed diet, but insects are the principal fare. The males are brightly colored in the breeding season; at that time the ordinary, mottled, gray-green body becomes ornamented, especially in the neck region, with shades of orange, blue, yellow, and brown. This lizard is more or less common over the entire southwestern desert area.

The flat-nosed horned lizard (*Phrynosoma platyrhinos*), with short head-spines, is the only horned lizard of the Mohave region. On the Colorado Desert we find, with it, the flat-tailed horned lizard (*P. m'callii*), a species armed with large head-spines and with ashy-gray body bearing a narrow but distinct line down the center of the back. The food of these squat reptiles consists of insects, among which ants are a favorite. During the coolest months of the year they secrete themselves in the sand and go into a short period of hibernation.

At least several of our terrestrial lizards possess a pair of salt glands, dorso-lateral in position, which open directly into the nasal cavity. Through these, excess salts taken into the body in their food can be voided. Insect-eating lizards build up large accumulations of potassium salts because insects contain these salts in large quantities. But it is not only the carnivorous lizards that have salt glands: some of the vegetarian species such as the chuckawalla have them too.

Not long will you wander about before you see living specimens or at least old bleached pieces of the bony carapace of the desert tortoise (*Gopherus agassizi*). Time was when this reptile was common in the Salton Basin; this is unhappily no longer the case. Their food is green plant material and this accounts for the apparent frequency of tortoises during the spring months. In winter as well as during the hottest summer months, they hide beneath rocks, or dig slanting burrows two or three feet deep in the sand. In the making of the retreat the earth is scraped loose with the forefeet, whereupon the animal turns around and pushes it out with its shoulders. To enable it to withstand periods of drought, the tortoise stores water in a pair of sacs situated between its flesh and its "shell." Numbers of tortoises are killed yearly by thoughtless motorists, and as many more are transported by curious folk to the coastal towns, where the animals live for awhile in their new environment and then often perish because of neglect. Desert tortoises are often now protected by law and cannot legally be taken or sold.

Said the late Angus M. Woodbury: "That lowly hard-shelled dweller of the Southwestern deserts is in serious danger of such depletion in numbers as to threaten extinction in many parts if not all of its range. In a ten-year study with Ross Hardy of tortoises in southwestern Utah, we found that it takes about 5 years after hatching for a young tortoise to develop a hard shell, about 15 to 20 years to reach maturity, and that the life span extends over a long period of time, perhaps as long as the human span.

"The rate of reproduction seems to be very low. A female may lay 3 to 7 eggs in early summer but how often they are produced in the life history was not determined. What proportion of these hatch is also not known, but it is certain that during the early years of life before the shell hardens, they are particularly vulnerable to predator attacks. I have seen a young tortoise that had been bitten in two by a predator. But even adults sometimes have their shells broken open and cleaned out by predators such as coyotes and wildcats.

"These are natural and normal losses to the tortoise population, to which the tortoise life history has become adapted over the ages. It is supposed that Indians and Mexicans have habitually used them for food. In desert areas, they would represent one of the largest food items obtainable by the aboriginal desert inhabitants and doubtless these losses would also be reflected in the adaptations of the tortoise to desert life."

Snakes are by no means common desert reptiles. They are found most often in the spring of the year, which is their mating season. A number of kinds are seen only at night, and this accounts for the scarcity of records of their occurrence. It is a great mistake to think that desert snakes are partial to sunshine and make no attempt to avoid the burning heat. Some of them, such as the horned rattlesnake, may be killed by even short exposure to the hot sun.

Sidewinder

Desert Boa

Pallid Rattlesnake

Red Racer

Mohave Rattlesnake

Great Basin Gopher Snake

The common olive-green rattlesnake of the open country of the Mohave Desert is the Mohave rattler (*Crotalus scutulatus*). It comes from its winter retreats early in March and is in evidence all through the summer. Its activities are not confined to the daylight hours; it crawls also at night, taking kangaroo rats and other small rodents which are then about. In the rock-mantled mountains of the northern Mohave Desert (Inyo, Coso, Panamint, Slate, Grapevine, and Funeral mountains) occurs the Panamint rattlesnake (*Crotalus confluentus stephensi*). The general ground color of this snake is tan, buff, or gray, with considerable variation occurring in the different mountain ranges; there is a beautiful patch of turquoise on the throat. As early as the last of March, individuals are out sunning themselves on the rocks.

The Texas rattlesnake (*Crotalus atrox*) is largely restricted to the Coachella and Imperial valleys and the region along the Colorado River near Yuma. It is a grayish or yellowish-brown species inhabiting the sandy-bottomed basins. In the rocky, mountainous areas in this same region the big speckled rattlesnake (*Crotalus mitchelii*) is encountered. This snake is also a Mohavean species. It occurs, too, in chaparral and oak country of the coastal areas.

Both in the broad, unicolorous, sandy basins and on the stony deserts of low altitude, the little horned rattlesnake or sidewinder (*Crotalus cerastes*) must be reckoned with by those travelers who roam about or camp on the desert at night. During the daytime this small but hot-tempered snake lies coiled in pits of sand or in small depressions about the shady bases of bushes where it has protection from the inhospitable sun. About sunset it begins to wander extensively in search of its prey, which consists mostly of wild mice and lizards. It moves in a singular sidewise, looping manner and leaves behind a series of telltale J-shaped tracks in the loose soil. I often have been surprised to find sidewinders out on cold, windy days of early March and mid-November, weather which to other reptiles is most discouraging to activity. They spend a short period in hibernation.

Excepting the red racer and the desert gopher snake, few of the snakes listed as nonpoisonous are seen alive by the average traveler. The desert burrowing snake, the patch-nosed snake, the California boa, the Western blind snake, the coach-whip striped racer, the leaf-nosed snake, the shovel-nosed snake, and the California lyre snake are sometimes seen dead on the highways, the victims of automobiles. Many of these snakes are active only at night.

8. Birds

Throughout the spring flower season the whole desert country is one broad food table for the birds. The tired bird-migrants, stopping for a few days' rest at the springs before going farther north, feed fat on the insects and ripening seeds, while the native nesting birds, assured of a full larder on which to draw while hatching their eggs and feeding their young, are busy preparing nests or engaging arduously in nursery duties. It is a fact well worth noting that during the drought years when there is little promise of food supplies, many desert birds, such as the insect-eating cactus wren and the thrashers, full of avian wisdom, nest early, or cut down the number of eggs, or forgo both nesting and egg laying, passing over the season without offspring.

About the springs and the small streams which trickle from them, one quickly ceases to be surprised at new bird visitors. A position of great advantage to the watcher of birds is the lone spring with its overhanging willow or two affording some semblance of protection to small birds from their rapacious and unloved brothers, the hawks. Twenty or more different kinds of birds a day in the month of April (the height of the migratory season) constitute no small list of water-hole visitants, yet the bird lover frequently sees that many. A good big pillow to lean the elbow on, some lunch, a pair of eight-power field glasses, and a large share of patience make a combination that surely brings great rewards. Goldfinches (the willow, the Lawrence, and the greenback), house finches, house wrens, mourning doves, mockingbirds, Alaska yellow warblers, hermit thrushes, and even the ever-contented red-shafted flicker are sure to be seen sooner or later. Running about on the rocks, almost like a mouse, that voluble, merry, scale-running songster, the canyon wren and its near-relative, the less musical but persistently singing, joyous-hearted rock wren, are perhaps watching for insects and spiders, quite oblivious or at least inattentive to their many bird neighbors below. By late April the sky is emptied of most of the fleeting migrants and there are left such hardy, endemic birds as the Say's phoebe, the raven, the roadrunner, the horned lark, the Gambel quail, the white-rumped shrike, the verdin, the plumbeous gnatcatcher, and the Le Conte and Crissal thrashers, those true sons of the desert which are able to go for long periods without dipping their beaks in water. In certain seasons some of the birds that are seed-eaters depend largely for their supply of moisture on the water found in the leaves of succulent plants or berries. Others, like the raven and the roadrunner, get quantities of water from the bodies of lizards and dead rabbits; but most of them secure water by eating insects or by elaborating it in their own bodies through the processes of metabolism. The amount of this metabolic water is probably not great, certainly not as great as develops in many of the rodents. Most birds take water at the springs and rivers when they can procure it, but apparently are able to get along for fairly long periods without recourse to the watering places. It is always to be remembered, however, that birds are not infrequently aware of small sources of water of which their human admirers never know. Also, many of them travel longer distances to water than one would dare to expect. Bolster tells of the sand grouse (*Pterocles senegallus*), a bird of the bare

Old World deserts which needs daily supplies of water, breeding at least thirty miles from the pools from which it drinks.
The parents get water to their young by first drinking it, then
regurgitating it for them.

During the spring and late summer and autumn migration
many birds die of thirst because they cannot find along the
way water sufficient for their needs. The late summer period
is the most hazardous for them, for usually there is no green
food and many of the water sources are dry. Many of the migrants avoid some of the perils by traveling at night.

Birds must depend on evaporation of water through panting to prevent dangerously high body temperature, or to keep
cool they may cut down their activities and seek the shelter
of shade or of deep rock crypts. Water loss by evaporative
cooling (panting) is comparatively high.

In maintaining water balance, birds have at least one very
distinctive advantage over mammals. As a means of saving
water they secrete nitrogen mostly as uric acid, which can be
voided in a semisolid state. Mammals secrete nitrogen in the
form of urea, which must be in a watery solution.

The few marshes and the narrow, muddy margins of the
isolated springs, lakes, and rivers offer attractions to many
of the wading birds. Terns, stilts, avocets, grebes, kingfishers,
cormorants, ibises, and many kinds of ducks in their season
of migration are drawn by the opportunity to feed and rest
in such agreeable surroundings as they find at Saratoga
Springs, by the Salton Sea, and along the bottoms of the Colorado River.

The large Great Basin Canada goose winters in the Imperial Valley in surprising numbers, the greatest concentra-
tions being seen on the lands surrounding the southeastern
end of the Salton Sea. From their breeding ground in northern states and Canada these graceful "flying honkers," as
they are often called, migrate in spectacular formations, eventually to alight on Wildlife Management waters and sur-

rounding fields where they rest and feed. It is a thrilling experience to watch these big birds (weighing up to twenty pounds) as they come in to rest, moving in lofty circles and at last settling, all the time trumpeting in unison. Another large bird found simultaneously from November to March with the Canada goose is the snow goose, which may occur in almost equal number (10–20,000); but the two kinds of birds do not mix.

Many other water birds may be seen to advantage in the Imperial Valley Wildlife Management Area and a visit there at any time of the year is a rewarding experience. A resident year-round keeper is in charge.

The great, domed saltbushes of the Salton Sink offer such ideal shelter and feeding grounds for the roadrunner that I am always sure of a sight of half a dozen or more of these amusing birds in any morning's ramble there. One of the cleverest exhibits of roadrunner sagacity that I have seen occurred one winter some years ago. Approaching one of those dried mud puddles of the roadside so common near Mecca, I saw George, as I like to call him, turning over the big mud plates which, curled up about the edges, lay all over the surface of the old mud pool. Catching hold of them with his beak, he turned them up on end, and over, all the time on the lookout for crickets and other insects lying hidden beneath. It was evidently an old trick of his, for almost all the mud plates on that and another pool had been turned.

In company with two of my students I once saw, on a midsummer morning's jaunt, a roadrunner making great haste to get to the shelter of a creosote bush. Two somber-colored marsh hawks were after him. Contrary to what I expected, the hawks lighted on the ground and began making repeated dives into the creosote bush. The roadrunner did not long stay under cover, for he was no coward. A moment later we saw him become the aggressor in the struggle. There began a merry tussle, both hawks and roadrunner going in more or less merry-go-round fashion around the bush, the hawks rather awkwardly, the roadrunner very gracefully, and as if enjoying the contest enormously. At length one of the hawks retreated to some distance, but the other flew away and alighted under a nearby creosote bush. George immediately pursued him, for he was not through with his fun, and there began all over again the ludicrous dodging and running back and forth around the bush. Finally outdone in the contest of wits, the last hawk disgustedly flew away. The triumphant roadrunner, with head held proudly aloft and with a clipping of its bill, ran off unconcernedly at top speed.

Gambel Quail   Roadrunner   Scott Oriole   Desert Sparrow

The small ladder-backed or Texas woodpecker is a noisy little fellow, often calling in high-pitched notes as he flies in undulating sweep from bush to bush. Before the advent of civilization he drilled his nest holes in the tree yuccas, in cactus stems, and in branches of larger trees when he could find them. With the coming of the railroads and the power lines, he found new materials for his beak to drill in. The erection of telegraph, telephone, and power-line poles was a stroke of good luck. He at once took to drilling so many holes that he made himself a creature of concern. Thousands of poles have been ruined by his innocent work.

Except perhaps for a few weeks in the spring when there are succulent plants in abundance and quantities of berries on the bushes of the wild Lyciums, the Gambel quail prefers to be a daily drinker and thus stays rather close to springs and streams. Occasionally, however, one sees quail so far from known water holes that one wonders what sources of water they can have. This handsome bird is found not only on the desert floor but also in the stony canyons high up among the junipers and piñons.

In the piñon–juniper woodlands of the high desert, especially in autumn, one may come upon small to large flocks of the uniformly gray-blue piñon jay. Except during the nesting season, they are nomadic, gregarious, and noisy birds. Emitting a persistent high, quavering nasal caw, they fly about trying to keep in constant contact with other members of the moving flock.

Another interesting avian resident is the buoyantly flighted Say's phoebe, a flycatcher of gray-brown color with rusty underparts. It is one of the few birds to be seen in the lowest parts of Death Valley and other places where the more extreme types of desert conditions prevail. Early in the morning, long before the sun is up, its plaintive and haunting but forceful songs are heard in great numbers. As soon as it is light enough for the birds to see, there is a noticeable surcease of song. Then for an hour or more they are busy foraging for insects, making repeated sallies from some isolated cliff or fence post out into mid-air to capture their flying breakfast. But before the morning is half over the songs begin again. The birds continue their calls until evening, except at noonday, when they take refuge from the heat under bushes or rock ledges. Almost every abandoned miner's shack has its phoebe's nest on some rafter. The nest, also frequently built on the ledge of an abandoned mine shaft, is made of old string, grass, and bits of paper. A pair of the birds once nested for me in a rusty stovepipe; this they half filled with bits of string and manure. It was on the sunny side of the house and in the month of May. How the birds kept themselves from roasting alive is still a mystery to me.

At several of the desert oases such as China Ranch, Camp Cady on the lower Mohave River, Twentynine Palms, and Big Morongo, bird watchers from time to time excitedly report seeing the handsome vermillion flycatcher. In some of these places it is known not as a migrant or a vagrant but as a nesting species. This small flaming-red flycatcher is a quite common nester in the trees along the Colorado River in March and April.

The handsome Brewer blackbird, partial to cultivated areas, is a winter visitant in the southeastern deserts. Its somewhat near relative, the dwarf brown-headed cowbird, is permanently resident over the entire area from Death Valley southward where they stay near sources of water. The male may be distinguished from the blackbird by its smaller size, brown head and sparrowlike, conical beak. The red-winged blackbird is a desert dweller only in well-watered places such as we have in irrigated portions of Imperial Valley and fields along the Colorado and Mohave rivers.

To that stolid old-gentleman-tramp of the railway and highway right-of-way, the raven, time is no object. Even during the scorching days of summer, he and his mate may be seen walking or flying with a businesslike demeanor up and down the highways or the railroad tracks, alert for morsels discarded from lunch baskets or for small animals killed by passing cars. At times the raven seems a dull, inactive creature, but he really has a great share of curiosity and something of a sense of humor; I believe his ways deserve careful study. It is noteworthy that this sagacious bird, though so large, has been able to survive his many persecutors. On the rocky deserts he gets his supplies of water by eating insects, birds' eggs, lizards, or the carcasses of rabbits that have been killed on the highways. It is probable that along the Colorado River he not only gets a good drink but also a fish occasionally. Ravens are most often seen in pairs except when the young are consorting with their parents. There are no crows on our deserts.

The European house sparrow, our almost universal bird scamp, has followed the sun westward and penetrated even to the bottom of Death Valley. There he chirps disquieting songs to the small birds which with him seek protection under the downhanging leaves of the Washingtonia palms at Furnace Creek Ranch. The European house sparrow has this redeeming trait: he confines himself to the vicinity of human habitations.

Among the really fine singers of spring is the desert or black-throated sparrow. His song is a quaint but cheerful and far-carrying melody, *tsee tsi tsi tsi tsee* or *weet weet wee,* the last note held and almost trilled. Approach him closely and you can see his well-defined black chest and chin and the distinctive clean white lines above and below his eye. The nest, built of plant fibers, is placed in low shrubs or in crotches of the spiny opuntias.

Like a glad harbinger of the glorious sunny winter days to come, the Gambel white-crowned sparrows appear from the north early in November to make their home in the Salton Sink. The birds are soon everywhere, filling the air with their simple and cheerful songs, sometimes seeming to sing in chorus. They are joined soon after by Audubon warblers, by Western or mountain bluebirds, robins, house finches, and a host of obscurely marked sparrows such as the sage sparrow

and the bell sparrow. We see many of the sparrows consorting in flocks to go wheeling about in the air or gathering in
small groups to feed in very businesslike manner about the
bases of bushes where seeds of the summer's ripening have
been collected by the winds. Some days when storms occur in
the mountains, Thurber juncos and Bailey chickadees come
down to join the merry company.

The large cactus wren, by reason of its clattering call notes
and queer, flask-shaped nests which it builds in cactus bushes
and in palo verde trees, is one of the most conspicuous of
desert birds. It is always interesting to examine a fresh nest
to see what plants have been chosen for use in its construc-
tion and decoration. The fine-stemmed eriogonums and the
woolly filagos and styloclines are almost always present; sometimes a few bright-hued blossoms are added to the outside,
apparently as a decoration.

Pleasant indeed it is to wake up in the morning and hear
the little rock wren merrily greeting the dawn with its absurd
but merry tinkling song. Watch persistently among the barren ledges of the rocky hills nearby and you will see it perched
on the summit of some boulder or spit of rock, bobbing up
and down like an ouzel. Later you may see the shy little creature retreating into piles of loose rocks, where it hunts its insect food and rears its young. If it is autumn its coat of brown
feathers will be much worn: a season of constant activity in
the rocky retreats has surely left its mark.

The most common hummingbirds of the winter and spring
season on the desert are the costa and black-chinned species,
the latter known only as a casual winter visitant of the Colorado Desert. They feed on nectar obtained from the blossoms of the bladder pod, chuparosa (sometimes called hum-
mingbird bush), and other plants with bright-colored tubular flowers. The rufous and some of the other Western hummingbirds may occasionally be seen in migration. In autumn
many of the bird perish while crossing the hot desert because
of the lack of nectar-yielding plants and insect food.

The desert claims the finest-singing and the handsomest of California's orioles. The trim black-and-yellow Scott oriole is a regular resident of the yucca forests of the Mohave Desert, and occasionally it is found flashing its brilliant form among the junipers. Its fibrous nest is fastened to the stiff spines of the yuccas. In the Colorado Desert the Arizona hooded oriole hangs its nest in the palms.

The little ball of gray twigs you so often see in the mesquite branches or in the spiny cat's-claw thickets is the nest of the tiny but active verdin. If the owner is anywhere about, you are certain to hear its insistent *tzee*-ing notes. Verdins always appear to be provident birds, and very much in earnest in whatever they do. Early in the season we see them engaging all their energies in collecting and bringing in the material for the new home. Often it is made from feathers and sticks from the previous year's nest. The male has the curious habit of building a separate sleeping nest. He is in some respects a lazy chap, and you will observe that his house is not so well constructed or so neatly furnished as the nest of his mate. In winter you may occasionally see him pop into his nest before sundown. Put your finger in through the small opening and you are certain to get a sharp pick. The verdin's yellow head, his chestnut-red shoulder patches, and the contrasting gray of the other parts of his body are field-marks matched by no other desert bird.

Often in small companies, but perhaps more frequently in pairs, the Yuma horned larks wander about in the open valleys, always protected by the plain browns and grays of their plumage. The furnacelike heat of glaring, alkaline plains and scorching sand dunes holds no terrors for them and we need not be surprised to find a female in late spring nesting in a depression of sand beside a clump of bunch grass and with nearly the minimum of shelter from the blazing sun. Disturb her and she flies a little way across the heat-scarred soil, circles around anxiously, and, with beak agape, soon returns and settles on her eggs.

The gnatcatchers, always hustling about in a great deal of excitement, are certain to claim our attention, particularly if it is early spring when they have nesting duties. The most common desert species is the lead-colored gnatcatcher, especially plentiful in the mesquite and ironwood thickets of the Colorado Desert. The call notes, a series of two or three short *chees,* are given as the birds in pairs work their way from bush to bush. One generally takes the lead, and the others, seemingly much excited, soon follow. The tail is never still but is continually flipped from side to side.

In the topmost twig of some mesquite or ironwood tree you are certain, sooner or later, to see that feathered bird-aristocrat, the glossy, black phainopepla. In all probability he will, by the motions of his proud head, display his fine black crest and scarlet eye or, flying gracefully upward after some insect, will reveal the remarkable white patches of the under wing-feathers. In the clump of mistletoe beneath him are those pearly-white or pinkish berries which he relishes above all foods. On twigs and on posts near at hand you see the evidences of his keen appetite, the high heaps of rejected, sticky seeds which passed undigested through his body.

The small, very active gray-backed, white-breasted Lucy warbler is a Colorado Desert summer visitant in California in the mesquite thickets of the lower Colorado River. It may also be found in similar situations in southern Utah, New Mexico, and Arizona. Since it is so closely associated with the mesquite where it feeds and builds its nest, it is often called the mesquite warbler.

Another feathered inhabitant that never seems to mind the heat is the neatly attired, white-rumped shrike. Were it not for his flattened head, which gives him the appearance of a creature of low intelligence, we should call him a handsome bird. From earliest dawn we hear his sharp cries, and if it is near the nesting season his song may have in it an element of beauty, for even this bird, which pins little birds on barbed-wire fences and mesquite thorns, is, in the days of his love, no longer the harsh-voiced fellow he was in late summer or winter. If you would have some real excitement mingled with an element of fun, hunt out a nest of young shrikes at just about the time that they are leaving it. The hubbub of excited cries and screeches from the baby birds and the noisy, daring dashes of the anxious parents, which seem ready to deliver stabs and blows fatal to the intruder, are impressive. Inasmuch as shrikes feed on insects and get most of their water from them, they are not dependent on the water holes and springs but scatter widely over the desert basins throughout the year.

Perhaps all through the night, especially in spring and summer, one hears the quaint and almost unceasing call notes of Nuttall's poorwill. This bird spends much of its time sitting on the ground, rising from time to time in fluttering fashion to snatch up in its widely gaping beak moths and other small nocturnal flying insects. If one approaches it at night with an electric torch, the eyes shine bright red.

It was the author's good fortune in the winter of 1946 to find, in a granitic crypt, one of these birds in a state of torpidity. It was banded for identification, and for several succeeding winters it returned to the same spot to sleep away the season of poor food supply. Studies and experiments carried on during this period confirmed belief that here is a bird that truly hibernates. It was a discovery of major importance to ornithologists. Since that time some thirty other poorwills have been found in a state of "winter sleep."

The wise traveler will always get up early in the morning with the rock wrens and catch the changing glories of the coming day. Also he will learn to spend the closing hours of the day in quietness so as to have full opportunity to watch the setting sun, the cloud forms which it gilds and reddens, and perchance to hear, in contrast to the intense stillness of evening, the clear, liquid notes of that magnificent bird singer of the mesquite country, the Le Conte thrasher. The song of this ashy-gray bird with its long curved beak is remarkable for the richness of its tone. It is much like that of the mockingbird but less formal. Quite in contrast is the call note or note of alarm, a sharp whistle—*whit*. This is the desert's shyest bird and when disturbed by an intruder it retreats with a fleetness that always surprises. It seldom leaves the ground, but runs from bush to bush in rapid zigzags. The nest, built in bushes or cactus patches, is almost invariably felted with filago, a downy little plant much prized by many desert birds as a nest lining.

Another curved-beak thrasher, darker than the Le Conte, is the Crissal, so called because of the chestnut crissum or undertail patch. It, too, is an excellent singer and particularly given to living in the dense brush thickets of mesquite, arrowweed, and quail brush that are found along the Colorado River.

Bendire's thrasher, with shorter almost straight beak, gray-brown back, and faint spots of brown on the lighter breast, is more apt to be found on the open desert. Peterson aptly describes its fine song as "a continuous, clear, double-noted warble not broken into phrases."

The small sage thrasher has a straight robinlike beak and very noticeable streaked breast. It is most common in the sagebrush areas of the Great Basin. In our low deserts it is seen only in migration.

Of the birds of prey, the spirited prairie falcon seems most typical of the desert. It nests on high cliffs, and the site of its home is easily detected during the nesting season by the piercing cries of the young and the wild, penetrating, distressful notes and daring, agitated flight of the parents.

The large and powerful Western red-tailed hawk is also a cliff nester, and we not infrequently see its large stick nests mounted high on the steep canyon sides. Reptiles are a part of this hawk's bill-of-fare, and in summer I have seen the birds flying with live snakes in their talons.

The handsome sparrow hawk is frequently seen sitting on posts. It probably subsists on grasshoppers as well as small insects.

The golden eagle, rather easily identified by its large size and dark feather coat, was once rather plentiful but has been severely reduced in numbers by thoughtless, ignorant, and often stupid hunters who wish to use every bird of prey, especially the larger ones, as a target.

Turkey vultures are also resident in the desert area, and in autumn they at times gather in great numbers to roost in the cottonwood trees along the Mohave River. Along with the crows and ravens, they are always attracted by the carcasses of dead rabbits on the highways. No one has a better opportunity to study the habits of vultures than the observing motorist. When disturbed, the birds unfold their wings and take off with a vigorous spring; a few hurried flaps carry them to safety, and soon they are seen circling high in air, their wings set to the wind.

The intense and impressive stillness of the desert night is frequently broken by the wild, deep, measured notes—*whoo, hu-hoow, whoo, whoo*—of the horned owl. In the breeding season these notes are supplemented by a variety of other sounds, and if the birds happen to be perching on rocks near your desert camp you will be quite convinced that they are very noisy lovers. In spring, the ear often catches other bird songs at night. I have repeatedly heard mockingbirds, linnets, and desert sparrows bubble over in erratic song long after dark.

In your daytime wanderings along tree-lined sand washes you may chance to see a long-eared owl sitting stolidly among the tree branches and almost invisible. It is a small owl readily identified by its two long, upright ear tufts.

You infrequently may see, while sauntering over the open deserts, singly or in pairs the ludicrously long-legged ground or johnny owl. Nearby will probably be the entrance to the underground burrow. If you approach closely, the small, large-headed owl will probably flutter off to some distance and, coming to a stop, engage in strange head-turning and bobbing motions.

9. Mammalian Life

The desert's mammalian fauna is represented by thirty-six genera comprised of fully seventy-five species and subspecies. It is most interesting to note that at least two-thirds of the various mammals found on deserts belong to the order of rodents or gnawing animals. Of these rodents it has been the mice and their near-relations that have been most successful, probably because they are, for the most part, burrowers that live on seeds and grasses and are not dependent on ordinary sources of water for drink. They may be classed along with the hares and ground squirrels among the "savers." Few if any of them perspire, most of them pass scant amounts of urine, and many drink no water from the day of birth to the day of death, their dependence for water being placed wholly on the free water in their food and the water elaborated through the processes of metabolism. The average traveler is largely unaware of the presence of these animals, for they are active mostly at night. But if he is at all circumspect in his observations he will at least see the results of their active labors in the myriads of little holes and scratchings, to say nothing of the many lacelike patterns left in the sands by their countless journeys in search of seeds.

"One might," says Tristram, commenting on the rodents

of the desert region adjacent to Palestine, "easily be accused of exaggerating in describing the countless number of holes and burrows in the regions which, for the greater part of the year, present features of utter desert. Sometimes for miles a region has the appearance of one vast warren of pygmy rabbit holes: yet for days, saving the bounding of a jerboa [a small, fawn-colored, jumping rodent] before one's horse, not another trace of rodent life is to be seen."

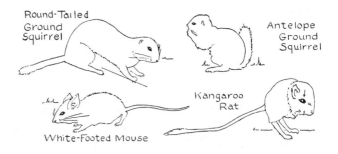

Round-Tailed Ground Squirrel

Antelope Ground Squirrel

Kangaroo Rat

White-Footed Mouse

In the sand dunes, where digging is easy, almost every strong-rooted bush and tree has its kangaroo rat holes with well-beaten runways leading in all directions to the feeding grounds. If the sands have been long undisturbed by winds, they may contain many visible records of the merry waltzings and spirited hops and quarrels these animals engage in during the nocturnal hours.

One traveling over sand thickly occupied by kangaroo rats is certain to find himself all of a sudden in a foolish and laughable situation, for while he walks the ground suddenly begins to give way beneath him as the ceilings of numerous burrows cave in, and he reels like a drunken man in an earthquake. Every step forward sends him into new ludicrous positions; he may even fall headlong and go sprawling on the earth. Just about the time he feels that he has reached solid ground, down he goes again and he begins to wonder if there is any end to the extensiveness of the honeycomb of underground passages. I once saw a pack burro venture into such a place; the animal became so frightened that it could never be induced to try it again; in fact, it was ever afterward suspicious of any ground that sounded hollow beneath.

If a tapping sound is made at the mouth of one of the numerous burrows, the animals within are likely to respond with a sound described by a well-known naturalist as having a churring or fluttering quality and resembling the noise of flying quail. It is probably a signal of alarm or note of challenge made with the hind feet striking repeatedly and rhythmically against the sands. Trade rats when annoyed respond in the same way over and over again.

Dr. Schmidt-Nielsen of Duke University has recently done some most interesting and significant work on the water requirements and water utilization of kangaroo rats. It has long been known that these arid-land rodents seldom drink free-water but depend largely upon "biologic water" derived from the chemical breakdown of their food. Their kidneys are about four times as efficient as the kidneys of man in removing nitrogenous wastes (urea) from the blood, hence they use comparatively less water. Kangaroo rats have no sweat glands so there is no water loss through perspiration. Body water is further conserved by confining the feeding and other activities to the cool night hours when humidity is highest. Like many of the desert rodents, they spend their daytime in underground retreats where humidity is higher than in the moisture-hungry dry air above ground.

Dust bathing among kangaroo rats is frequent. This keeps the fur largely free from oils secreted by the large glands on the back between the shoulders. Captive kangaroo rats denied dusting privileges soon have matted fur; they become listless and ill, and finally die. If supplied with dust, the sick animals immediately begin dust bathing and soon recover their sleek fur and good health. The desert kangaroo rat with white-tipped tail is largest of the kangaroo rats and lives in areas of deep sand. The large-eared piñon mouse is widespread on our deserts. The pale-gray cactus mouse is fairly common, too, especially on low deserts where cacti abound.

There is scarcely a square mile of the desert, with the exception of the dry lakes, that does not have its share of white-footed mice.* These dainty, big-eared creatures are found poking their noses into every possible rock cleft and beneath every succulent herb or bush. In winter they find their way into the settlers' cabins, stealing wads of cotton from the unprotected mattresses and getting into the supply cans unwittingly left open; in fact, they turn everything they explore or discover topsy-turvy and leave a sad mess of shredded papers, chewed rags, and tattered bags as evidence of their winter's occupation.

The grasshopper mice live such obscure and hidden lives

---

* Dr. F. B. Sumner has made extensive studies of the way in which the colors of these mice vary with the colors of their environment. Like many other desert animals, the desert races of white-footed mice (*Peromyscus*) are usually much paler than those dwelling in more humid localities. This has commonly been interpreted as an instance of concealing coloration, evolved as a means of protection. There is doubtless some truth in this view. But Dr. Sumner and others offer reasons for believing that an arid climate may result in the loss of dark pigment in the skin, regardless of the color of the background on which the animal chances to dwell. He found, for instance, that a large collection of skins of a certain white-footed mouse living upon an area of black lava in the Mohave Desert displayed the characteristic pallor of desert races in general, and further he found that the color of these mice agreed very closely with that of a collection of the same species taken upon pale gray, buff, or pinkish rocks. Thus the precise correspondence between the color tones of the animal and those of its immediate background seems to have been overemphasized by some writers. On the other hand, the fact that pale races of mice occur on some of the isolated beaches of Florida, where there is high atmospheric humidity, is evidence that concealing coloration, achieved through natural selection, is one factor in the evolution of such races. Dr. Sumner expresses the belief that both these agencies—the physiological effect of low atmospheric humidity and the selection of inconspicuous variations—have probably worked together toward producing the characteristic hues of desert mammals and birds.

that few people are ever aware of their existence. They are robust little fellows with short, thick tails and velvety fur. They live in burrows dug in the sand, and in these retreats lay up their small stores and build their nests of vegetable fibers. One of the chief items of their bill of fare is insects; grasshoppers and crickets are their favorites. The wide variety of other animal food, dead birds, lizards, and scorpions, is supplemented by many kinds of seeds. "At night," says Vernon Bailey, "their presence is often made known by a firm, prolonged whistle, so sharp and shrill as to suggest the sound produced by some insect."

Harvest mice, the smallest of our desert mammals, live in the clumps of grass and weeds about the springs. They subsist chiefly on seeds. Their little ball-shaped nests are built above ground under cover of bushes and in grass tussocks. It is to these small beasts that we credit many of the tiny well-worn paths that run from place to place in the weed tangles. The color of the harvest mouse above is dark buffy-gray, that of the under parts light gray. If you would be sure of your identification you must have a specimen in hand and look for the deep groove running down the front of each upper incisor tooth.

The acquisitive habit, so necessary to the welfare of the animals living in an arid country where harvests are far between, is seen to perfection in the little spiny pocket mouse. Nature intended him to be a collector, for she gave him a pair of cheek pouches to serve as pockets in which to carry to his home underneath the rocks the winter stores of seeds. If you would know this sociable little rodent, establish your winter camp near a mountain with rocky slopes plunging steeply into the level sands of the desert floor. The chances are good that on the very first night in the flickering light of your campfire you will catch sight of the tiny, spiny-backed creature popping about on the ground and picking up crumbs from beneath your camp table. He is no bigger than a walnut, yet he can leap two or three feet with the ease of a kangaroo. Watch his tiny front feet move with the speed of a shuttle as they cram his little cheek pouches to fullness. No sooner has he made away with a load than he is back again, busier than ever. Above all things he is fond of butter, and I have had him more than once sit on my knee to nibble some from the end of my extended finger. You may talk about him as you please, but he completely ignores your presence; make the smallest movement of head, foot, or hand, however, and he is off in a flash. Continually menaced by the silent owls, the foxes, and the sidewinders, he is alert to every movement. He knows full well that his safety lies in reaching his hole among the rocks.

Wherever there are rocks and sticks you will come upon the trash-pile nests of the desert wood rats; old cabins, abandoned mine tunnels, caves, and brushy areas are alike popular resorts of these ambitious hoarders. Sharing equal honors in mischief with the white-footed mice, they are the despair of the prospector who lives in a shanty. All night long they are busy carrying to their nests anything they can seize; at making queer thumping and scratching noises they are prize winners. Even in the open they are troublesome, for if you camp anywhere near their homes they are certain to pay you a visit before long, and if they don't steal any of your effects they are sure to disturb you by their endless gnawings. I always inspect ironwood trees and mesquite thickets for nests before camping near them. The common wood rat over most of the Southeastern desert is the desert neotoma. Along the Colorado and Mohave rivers are subspecies of the dusky-footed brush rats, which build cone-shaped houses of dead sticks in brush and against tree trunks. Up in the desert mountains the neotomas often build, decorate, and protect their homes with freshly cut twigs of the juniper.

Several kinds of mosquitoes have been observed hibernating in the food and dung chambers of wood-rat "nests." It is suspected that at certain times the females get blood from the rodents, especially from the young.

The brush lodges of the brown-footed wood rat are good places to hunt for spiders and phalangids. Dr. Raymond Ryckman and Robert D. Lee of Loma Linda University report finding spiders of seventeen different families in Southern California in the "nests" of brown-footed wood rats. This wood rat (*Neotoma fuscipes*) inhabits the coastal and foothill brushlands and in a number of places (see p. 104) invades the desert.

That little chipmunk-like creature with white tail held well over his back that scurried across the road and into the bushes as you approached was not a chipmunk as you suspected, but rather a miniature antelope ground squirrel.* You must expect to meet him almost everywhere you go. His scientific generic name, *Ammosphermophilus,* means "lover of seed and sand," and the specific name, *leucurus,* has reference to the white tail. This little ground squirel, or "ammo" as he is sometimes called, has a voice which for volume befits an animal ten times his size. The call is a long-continued, high-pitched, quavering trill and is most often heard in the mornings of spring. The young are absurd little midgets, "quiet as death," but interesting pets.

The antelope ground squirrel's nearest desert relative is the plain, light gray, round-tailed ground squirrel. This rodent is largely confined to the areas of drifting sands. He, too, is a small fellow, who comes out in the daytime but is by no means so commonly seen as his relative with the loud stripes. He likes the succulent herbs, and in spring he eats until his little belly almost bursts. Though reputed to be a vegetarian, this squirrel sometimes feeds on his dead mates and on rabbits crushed by passing autos. He makes his burrow in the sands, being careful if possible to get it under some

---

* The chipmunk's stripes run up to the point of the nose; those of the ground squirrel end at the shoulder.

protecting root where the coyotes and kit foxes cannot easily dig him out.

The Western cotton rat is an animal seldom seen but often found by the trapper on the flats along the lower Colorado River. Evidence of his occupation of an area is seen in the little piles of cut willow twigs and nibbled tules on the sand under the food plants.

The burrowing activities of pocket gophers are marked by the many fan-shaped mounds of loose earth which they push up from beneath the soil surface. The species occupying the delta soils of Imperial Valley is quite a different animal from the gopher of the opposite side of the Colorado River in Arizona and is also different from the very pallid Palm Springs gopher of the northwestern portion of the Colorado Desert. Because there are few places where the soil is sufficiently damp to work properly, gophers are necessarily among the rarer desert animals. The Botta pocket gopher is the widespread species of the arid Mohave and Colorado deserts. The Owens Lake gopher, a subspecies, is restricted to the immediate vicinity of the vanishing salina, and several others are peculiar to isolated desert mountains.

Sonoran beavers were once plentiful along the Colorado River, but they are now scarce because of the continual trapping. The dam-building habit, so common to the northern animals, has been given up by them, perhaps, as Dr. Grinnell has suggested, because of the unsettled behavior of the river and because there is sufficient natural falling of the green cottonwood trees to supply the immediate needs of bark for food. Small stick houses, felled trees, and well-marked tracks are occasionally seen.

The black-tailed jack rabbit or desert hare is perhaps the most frequently noticed larger mammal of the desert. The little Arizona cottontail is there too, but seldom crosses our path. So long are the legs of the jack rabbits that the animals look on first sight almost like small coyotes. I never tire watching them bound gracefully away, and I enjoy equally well a sight of them peacefully feeding or hiding under the brush or standing up on their haunches to get a broad view. And how clever they are at dropping their ears to protect the long appendages from injury when dashing under the thorny shrubs! Because of their habit of nibbling green crops, jack rabbits are the despair of the new settlers, and it is safe to say that these prolific animals have played an important role in helping to keep the desert the good wild place it was meant to be. Now and then the cacti feel the jack rabbit's sharp teeth and yield him an important supply of water.

The coyote is a perfectly typical wild dog. I sometimes feel that he has received, because of his howls, an almost undue amount of publicity. He speaks, it is true, in no uncertain sounds. His various wild calls to his mates as he goes out at evening time on the hunt are among the most fascinating of all the strange sounds that greet our ears. But the coyote has fallen on evil days. Relentlessly trapped and shot at by stupid gunners and killed by paid poison squads, he is no more king in his kingdom. We are genuinely sorry, because the coyote in his natural range is an animal worthy of our respect and admiration and an exceedingly valuable destroyer of noxious rodents. This wild dog has a reputation of being a coward, yet he is in fact a ferocious carnivore that pursues his prey with daring and skill. He brings great cunning to bear when hard after his fleeting meals. If you do not believe it, ask the jack rabbits.

The kit fox or desert swift is decidedly the most handsome of the larger mammals of the region. He is at once so graceful and so beautifully furred that a man who traps one should feel like a scoundrel for having brought misery and death to so fine an animal. Shy and timid in the daytime, he becomes bold at night, or perhaps we should say unsuspicious, and sometimes steals into our camp to pick up the scraps we always throw out to attract the wild creatures. The kangaroo rats of the dunes hold him no friend of theirs, for he is always appearing at the wrong time, breaking up their carnivals of play, and gobbling up the luckless ones for his midnight meal. Once plentiful, this splendid little fox is now fast disappearing over most of the desert area. Every autumn scores of shiftless trappers, thinking only of the few dollars they can get and possessing no regard for the welfare of the country's wildlife, run long steel-trap lines, some of them fully 200 miles long, and remain until late in the spring killing off every animal that can be baited. They leave the whole country a wreck insofar as wildlife is concerned. Their activities should certainly be curbed.

The kit fox's nearest kin in the desert area is the Arizona gray fox, a much larger animal of decidedly darker color. He is rather prone to stay in the hills and rocky canyons and leave the valleys and sandy flats to his smaller neighbor. On dark, cloudy days he may be out in the daytime a bit, but his regular hours for the hunt begin at dusk and last until dawn. Unsuspicious and often foolish, he stands a small chance against the wiles of his human persecutors.

The little spotted skunk is as handsome a beast as we see on the desert, and in spite of his regrettable habit of emitting an abominable-smelling fluid when he thinks his rights are invaded we give him almost first place among our favorite carnivores. He is really quite exemplary at minding his own business. By faithfully making his rounds over a wide area every night in search of wild mice and insects he gets a good living from the rocky country he inhabits. We regret that in his quest for something to eat he sometimes sets his paw in a trap. The hydrophobia skunk, as he is sometimes called, is no more guilty as a carrier of rabies than the coyote or any other desert animal. Skunks walk about on the palms of their hands and the soles of their little black feet after the fashion of bears. No kitten is more playful or dexterous with its paws. The big Arizona striped skunk is largely confined to the thickets along the Colorado River, kept there because of its daily need for water.

The desert has its own raccoon. Along waterways in the Imperial Valley and along sloughs, ponds, and channels of the Colorado River occurs the pallid coon. He lives principally on the unfortunate fish left by the overflows and on such small mammals, frogs, and insects as he can get on the muddy margins of the pools. Ring-tailed cats belonging to the same animal family (*Procyonidae*) are rare inhabitants of our mountainous desert areas.

It is yet possible now and then to see a badger. Though always persecuted by man, who ought to be his best friend, the badger has managed to survive in some of the more remote, unsettled basins. Squat of form and awkward in gait, he always strikes me as the queerest-looking animal I meet on my travels. The badger's home is a deep hole in the ground, placed, if possible, under the protecting roots of some sturdy shrub. His strong, well-clawed limbs enable him to do the excavating in a hurry once he starts the task. A former favorite sport of the cattlemen was to lasso the badger, let him get into his hole, and try to pull him out. The appetite of this carnivore is enormous. "Almost the whole life of the badger," says Vernon Bailey, "is spent in digging out the various rodents that constitute his food. It requires two or three fat ground squirrels, or a few gophers and a dozen mice, every day, to keep a badger in good condition."

In their hunting expeditions, wildcats wander widely and are always bobbing up in the most unexpected places. When in their new coat of winter fur they are good-looking animals, but by the end of winter the coat of gray, brown, and black is ragged and dirty. Wildcats hunt both by night and by day, and in their excursions through the brush they catch birds, rabbits, and other small mammals. The desert lynxes show the same tendency toward paleness of color found in so many desert animals. I cannot believe that pallor of coat originated in this animal as a protective character, for the wildcat has few natural enemies other than man.

Black-tailed deer wander far out over the arid mountains in the winter and sometimes descend into the warm desert valleys where there are springs. In late autumn, deer in numbers from the cold, high Sierra make the long journey across Owens Valley to the Death Valley region where they can enjoy a warm winter. I have several times in winter found them seeking water at springs in the barren mountains east of the Salton Sea. In years past the big-eared burro deer was found along the Colorado River bottoms, but I have heard of only a few small groups in recent years. It has gone the way of the antelope, which was once plentiful, especially on the mesas of the Mohave Desert.

I have already dwelt at length in my former books, *Denizens of the Desert* and *Desert Wildlife,* on the habits of the noble desert bighorn, and I shall let the reader seek more information about him there. It is a shame that this fine animal has not been better protected. He has held his own against the hunters longer than we had expected. Go to his haunts, reader; see him; but please be half a man and do not shoot! In spite of some so-called "official reports" in which the sheep are numbered by several thousands, I am constrained to affirm there are no more than eight or nine hundred sheep left in all the desert ranges of California. If they were even one-half as plentiful as some selfish interests proclaim them to be, it would be easy to see sheep everywhere. Most of those who observe carefully do well to see a few, except in guarded reservations, in two or three months or even in as many years.

California's magnificent tule elk has now become an established part of the fauna of the desert area of the lower part of the Owens Valley. The animals were introduced there in 1933. This is the smallest North American elk. The herd here of about 300 animals and several small groups totaling about 100 animals are all that remains of a vanishing species once abundant in the San Joaquin Valley. The Society for the Preservation of the Tule Elk is making a noble and determined effort to have a large and permanent reserve established in lower Inyo County where the animals can be kept inviolate from the interference of cattlemen and game hunters.

On wide elastic wings millions of bats emerge silently from the deep rock crevices and old mines at early dusk. They come out with empty stomachs and soon are wheeling about, hawking for insects. Often on moonlight nights I have lain awake and watched them swinging their way back and forth above my head.

The first bat to appear after dark is a little *Pipistrellus*. It is a bat of swift and erratic flight, flying high against the sky, but it may sometimes be seen abroad before sunset and in the morning after sunrise. Later in the evening the little buff-colored pallid bat comes forth and begins flying in low zigzag manner above the low bushes, but seldom appears above the skyline.

The shrill cicadalike note of the pale lump-nosed bat may be heard all through the night. This bat is called the burro bat by the miners because of its long ears and also the lump-nosed bat because of the peculiar glandular swelling on the sides of its nose. It roosts in the daytime in tunnels and caves throughout the desert area.

The spotted bat belongs to a genus (*Eudermia*) confined wholly to southwestern United States. It was once described by a desert resident as a large bat "with ears like a jackass and a white stripe on each shoulder." He might well have mentioned in addition the white patch on its rump and its remarkably furless, parchmentlike wings and tail membrane.

10. The Aborigines of the Desert

Some of the earliest reliable and important evidence of ancient man's occupancy of our California deserts comes principally from four areas: (1) Pinto Basin, at the eastern end of the Joshua Tree National Monument; (2) Lake Mohave, now Soda Lake; (3) Little Lake, south of Owens Lake; (4) Lake Manix and vicinity, east of Daggett. All the discoveries of stone instruments, bone fragments, and pieces of pottery and other evidences (geological and archaeological) indicate that man occupied stream- and lake-side sites in these areas as long as 9,000 or 10,000 years ago.

As post-Pleistocene conditions brought about the geographical expansion of arid territory in the Southwest, the "desert tradition" aboriginal cultures arose. Some peoples developed "sedentary cultures" such as those possessed by the ancient Anasazi (ancestors of the present-day Hopi), Hohokam, and Mogollon peoples of Arizona and New Mexico. These arid-land dwellers were primarily horticulturists: they had permanent dwellings and engaged in the manufacture and use of pottery. Always inventive, they learned to cultivate beans, squash, and better and better kinds of corn, which probably were brought in from Mexico. Other occupants of arid lands of the Southwest became nonagricultural wanderers: they

made no permanent dwellings, only temporary shelters. Most
of their time was spent circumventing starvation by foraging
for herbs, roots, berries, bulbs, and seeds. California's early
arid-land occupants fit into this latter category. Some excep-
tions were the semisedentary Colorado River people and
those who dwelled about the borders of lakes.

It is indeed to their credit that they survived in a land so
impoverished. They are an outstanding example of the way
a primitive people will make the best of an environment, doing amazing things with the little that apparently is there.

Excluding some Colorado River groups, most of the California desert Indians developed basket making to the point
of a fine art; also, they made woven seed beaters by means of
which they could gather seeds of grasses, annual herbs, and
shrubs. At a much later date some of the nonsedentary peoples began in a limited way to make and use simple pottery
vessels, most of them undecorated, for cooking, storage, and
the transporting of water. Their large round ollas may still occasionally be found where they cached them in rock shelters,
and pieces or potsherds of various vessels are strewn along
the old trails and about ancient campsites near water holes.

Special emphasis on particular material items including
clothing of course varied from people to people. Arid-region
men sometimes wore breechcloths and many women wore
two-piece bark-cloth skirts; others, especially men, simply
went naked, donning a rabbit-skin robe or shawl when in-
clement weather dictated. Some of the Northern Paiutes wore
skin moccasins; others wore skin-soled sandals. Most of these
Indians of the interior desert places wore a sandal made of
coarse fibers, usually yucca fibers.

Almost without exception, both lowland and highland Indians of California cremated their dead and burned the
houses of the deceased, leaving little behind. The most permanent human artifacts are, of course, the ones most commonly found—stone mortars and pestles, occasionally pot-

tery, and some beads and primitive jewelry. In dry, much sheltered places, some centuries-old perishable goods like baskets and seed beaters have been found.

Petroglyphs or animal pictures, signs and symbols incised on dark rocks, are another clue to early human occupation of California's desert regions. When these pictures or symbols are painted on rocks (sometimes in more than one color) they can be called pictographs. These are far less common than petroglyphs, and they are usually done on lighter-colored rock. The significance of these rock designs is left largely to conjecture, but a good guess is that they are records of important events made by several people at different times of occupation. It is thought that here we may have evidence of a belief in "imitative magic" to ensure good hunting and good crops, and that the petroglyphs and pictographs may have been an important part of ceremonial or religious rites.

Other scholars feel that these Indian "writings" were made by a primitive people who, quite like modern man, could not resist making some sign of his presence, or who made pictures simply to satisfy their desire to depict some happening or the form of something they had seen.

The petroglyphs of Little and Big Petroglyph Cañons, located on the north range of the United States Naval Ordnance Test Station north of China Lake community, comprise one of the largest groupings in California and probably the most spectacular in the United States. The glyphs, both varied and complex, are found on dark volcanic rock walls and are in good to excellent condition. The area has been designated as a national registered historical landmark. It may be visited only by permission.

The term tribe has all sorts of connotations, including that of a geographically unified group with a principal leader or chief. Of all the Indians of arid California, the Panamint or Koso Indians are the only ones actually close to being a "tribe." Almost all the others were scattered in small bands or land-use communities. More often than not, each community had leaders for each major activity: politics, warfare, hunting, etc. Although many of these local groups were quite unintelligible to one another, students of linguistics have recognized enough common language elements to group them conveniently and accurately into linguistic affiliations or stocks.

When the first Caucasians came into California they found the desert occupied by what have since been identified as two main linguistic stocks, the Shoshonean and the Yuman; the latter preceded by several hundred years the Shoshoneans in the arid regions around the Colorado River.

Along the rich bottom lands of the Colorado River, in what is now northeastern San Bernardino County, were the Yuman-speaking Mohave people. Hunting was of minor interest to them, but fishing, contrary to some earlier ethnological accounts, was of great importance. This food was supplemented by corn, squash, and beans. They made and used crude basketry and very simple pottery, which remained almost wholly functional, never becoming as elaborate as the earthenware of the later pueblo people to the northeast.

Although they were usually quite peaceful among themselves and frequently traded for rabbit-skin robes with the Walapai across the river, they often engaged in sanguinary warfare with some of their neighbors, especially the Arizona Maricopa and Halcidoma (who were later assimilated into Maricopa society after being driven out of the Parker area by both the Mohave and the Yuma). Individual fights, band squabbles, and group warfare were common among the Mohave, for both simple and complex reasons, one of which was the practice of taking young girls and young women as captives to serve as slaves.

From archaeological evidence we are led to believe that from about the tenth to the sixteenth century A.D. there was a branch of the Mohave people living to the westward along the borders of Soda Lake and other waters ponded in lakes along the course of the lower Mohave River (Cronise Lake, Lake Manix), all in what is now eastern San Bernardino County. Charred heaps of clam shells left in the bordering sands and fire-blackened stones along the old beach lines mark the sites of their camps. When encroaching aridity made the area unfavorable for further occupancy, they withdrew and settled alongside their more favorably situated brothers in the Colorado River bottomlands. But as late as 1776, Father Garcés, the early Spanish missionary, found Mohave still occupying some territory a considerable distance to the west of Soda Lake, also along the lower Mohave River.

Immediately to the south of the Mohave territory lived the semipeaceful Chemehuevi (Southern Paiute). In ancient times they were for the most part wanderers, scattered in small itinerant groups over the eastern half of the Mohave Desert from the Kingston Range southward through the Providence Mountains to what is now the southern San Bernardino County line. They have been described as perhaps "the most miserable Indians of the West," and they left few evidences of their presence other than various symbols and animal portraits incised in the surfaces of dark rocks of their wide, wild, and desolate home.

Sometime in the eighteenth century some of the Chemehuevi came to live along both sides of the Colorado River, for the most part concentrated in the valley that now bears their name. They also lived on Cottonwood Island, brought there by the Mohave people, according to their account. At times they sided with the Mohaves and Yumans in warring against their contiguous Arizona neighbors.

The Indians of Death Valley, always few in number, were called the Panamints (Koso) and were also of Shoshonean stock. Together with their Shoshonean neighbors they occupied a wide sector of the most arid, inhospitable parts of both eastern California and adjacent Nevada. They had migrated into Death Valley and environs from the north and east. Some of them dwelt around the few water holes in the Valley such as Tule Springs, Surveyors Well, and Mesquite Spring, as well as in some of the bordering canyons where there were both springs and shallow streams. Others dwelt around minor water sources to the west and northward.

Archaeological studies indicate that Indians were living in Death Valley at least 6,000 years before the Christian era. They were primarily hunters; a culture based on seed-gathering was not established until about the first century A.D., perhaps even as much as a thousand years later. Theirs must have been a life of real hardship, since they had to occupy almost their whole time in a constant search for food. In low portions of the Valley within mesquite thickets they gathered the heavy crops of mesquite bean pods and pounded them in wooden mortars to make a meal. About the only animal food they had other than insects, a few birds, and lizards was rabbits, pack rats, and other rodents. Most of the rabbits were taken at the time of their communal drives in autumn, when many men gathered to chase the animals against fencelike brush obstructions, where they beat them to death with clubs. The skins were taken to be tanned, dried, and cut into strands, later to be sewed into blankets and robes. For an average blanket about five feet square from thirty to fifty rabbit skins were needed. Most of the meat was eaten fresh, but some was dried and stored for winter. In late summer (September) trips were made to the surrounding mountains to gather crops of piñon nuts, part of which they ate on the spot and others they always stored for the winter. At certain times of the year many kinds of seeds were gathered with woven beating nets. Little that was edible escaped attention; in times of hardship even cactus joints were dried and later boiled and eaten.

North and west of the Panamint proper dwelt the main group of Koso people. They were among the westernmost of the Shoshones. They centered around the southern and eastern parts of Owens Lake, east of the Sierra Nevada, having boundaries quite indefinite.

They relied heavily upon their basketry, making pitch-covered water "jars," carrying nets, and food baskets. In general their habits were much like those of their Death Valley neighbors. They lived in barren valley land with stony soil. Their numbers must necessarily have been few. When the white men came, these people, like many other southwestern Indians, showed them desert trails and the water holes along the way. They made a further important contribution by demonstrating the use of many wild plants.

Almost equal in numbers to the Mohave Indians were the Yuma, who lived along the Colorado River and about the mouth of the Gila. Their territory was just to the south of that occupied most recently by the Chemehuevi. They were extremely mobile, traveling a great deal and doing a lot of trading. As far as economy and warfare were concerned they were almost identical with the Mohave, with whom they often sided in times of conflict with the Maricopa and Cocopah, who also were Yuman-speaking groups. In time they became embroiled in a war with the peaceful, sturdy-bodied Pima who lived in the valleys of the Gila and Salt Rivers. A great battle was fought in 1858, and the Yumas were almost annihilated.

The Cocopah lived to the south of the Yuma along the very lowest reaches of the Colorado River, i.e., near the upper Gulf of California. Many of them were in areas that are now part of Lower California and a few still live there. They lived in "puebloid" structures downriver as far south as places where the water became brackish. The name of this group is retained in the Cocopah Mountains, a desolate, rocky, and nearly waterless north and south range of Baja California some forty-five miles long.

All the natives dwelling along the Colorado River were

better off than their scattered desert-dwelling neighbors, for here was a dependable water supply as well as many annual and perennial plants which furnished them food and materials for housing. The river waters gave them fish for food, while otters and beavers supplied them with skins for clothing. Birds, lizards, and mammals, some as large as the burro deer, provided variety in their diet.

Among both the aboriginal and historical Indians were those who out of economic necessity or curiosity engaged in trade and traveled back and forth across country over well-chosen trails. Since it was their custom to make their trails wherever possible over the stony flatlands rather than in the sandy areas, their long, well-beaten, and stone-cleared pathways are still traceable in quite a number of places. It was customary among many of these people to place trail markers of stone or potsherds, or sometimes sea shells, where their trails crossed and at other intermittent significant points, so that in time there grew up little monuments. On the basis of present ethnological evidence, it seems likely that many of these were of religious significance, being trail shrines of a sort.

Two well-known trails were those going north and south along both banks of the Colorado River. Another very important trail was made by the Mohave Indians, who went to the west coast to procure sea shells which they could use in barter with their neighbors. To white travelers and explorers who later used it, it came to be known as the Mohave Trail. Another well-worn trail crossed in tortuous ways from Arizona to the Salton Sink, then northwestward to join the Mohave Trail somewhere near San Bernardino. There were many minor but well-marked trails between permanent water sources and the smaller trails over which the Indians went to the mountains to hunt (if they were not restricted by hostile groups already in occupancy) and to gather piñon nuts, bulbs, berries, and acorns.

When about A.D. 900 the Colorado River, running mean-
deringly over its deltaic cone, slipped westward and northward to discharge its waters into the Salton Basin again, it
created a large inland lake covering an erstwhile alkali- and
salt-covered ancient dry-lake bed. Geologists refer to this body
of water as the Blake Sea (named after the explorer W. P.
Blake, who first gave the Colorado Desert its name in 1853).
Almost immediately along the shores of this new, large fresh-
water lake there sprang up cattails, arrowweed, and other
water-loving plants, then later mesquite trees, and finally
palms. The Indians, especially the Yumans living along the
Colorado River, moved into this new desert paradise, established villages, and began fishing in the lake's waters. There
they stayed until the water, replenished only intermittently
by the fickle river, became undrinkable because of the high
concentration of salt brought about by the drying heat of
the desert sun and wind. They then moved back to their old
habitat next to the Colorado's mainstream. The upper end
of the Salton Basin, that is, the low-lying area north of the
Salton Sea, was occupied by another group, the Shoshonean
Cahuilla. Not unlike the other Indians of the region, they
were seed gatherers. In this sunken desert where ground water was in places fairly close to the surface, the honey and
screw-bean mesquite flourished and furnished much of the
staple food in the form of sweet beans. Where the Cahuilla
could find water at springs or obtain it by digging "walk-in"
wells, they made semipermanent settlements such as those at
Indian Wells and Agua Caliente. From these centers they
scoured the near and far country for food. Even today some
of their ancient gathering trails can be found in the bordering
mountains, some penetrating into the high mountains. Some
of the mortars they pecked in the rocks are still useable. The
Cahuilla were excellent basket makers and used pottery to a
greater extent than many of their neighbors; some of it was

decorated. Potsherds are sometimes fairly abundant along the old trails and in the sands about their former villages.

Other Indians of California's arid lands were the Vanyume and the Serrano. The Vanyume, now extinct, dwelt along the Mohave River. Garcés mentions them as occurring between Camp Cady and Daggett; also near Victorville. The Serrano were really mountain people, but they sometimes came down onto the Mohave Desert, as at Twentynine Palms, and at least temporarily dwelt there.

If you visit some of the groups of desert Indians as they are found today in the few reservations, you will see but the sad remains of an interesting civilization. A few old people can still tell you something of the ways of their ancestors, but most of the Indians have little real interest in their past. This is especially true of the younger people, who unfortunately have become very Americanized, dress in modern clothing, and live in unpicturesque houses built along white-man's style. Many have altogether forsaken their old home territories and now live among other races as town and city dwellers, their identity largely lost.

11. Botanical Aspects of Arid Regions

The remarkable vegetation of the desert areas of the world has received the attentive study of many botanists. Evidence of an early active interest in the flora of arid America is found in the reports of numerous explorers who traveled over the West in connection with various military and railway expeditions undertaken in the first three-quarters of the nineteenth century. In the appendices of the often bulky volumes we find beautifully wrought illustrations of the bizarre plants which pleased the eyes of such intrepid botanist-explorers as John C. Frémont, John Torrey, and Dr. Edward Palmer. The accounts of the journeys of these men form some of the most fascinating narratives in American literature; they verily make one travel-hungry. Few writings of the present are as vigorous or as refreshing in their descriptions of localities and of plants growing there.

Our desert's floral season is, on the whole, a short one, a show of wild beauty that lasts at best but six weeks or three months, from February through April or May. In ordinary years when winter and early spring rains are scanty, the annual flowering plants are few; and inasmuch as they are in no particular way adapted to endure shortage of water, they wilt and die a few weeks after they have sprung, as if by magic, from the barren earth. As though trying to make up for this poor showing, every few years comes an abundance of rain and there results such a wealth of blossoms that almost every foot of sand or gravelly soil is hidden beneath a blanket of flowers.

Gilias, desert primroses, phacelias, and various species of wild buckwheats and composites are among the commonest and most widely distributed of the annual plants. Where seeds of the previous seasons have lodged in the sands about the bases of the shrubs, myriads of these and other short-lived flowers spring up and form soft, flowery cushions whose appearance of luxuriance is much heightened by the intermingling growths of small grasses. In late spring the western rim of the Mohave Desert may be aglow with fields of Kennedy's mariposa (*Calochortus kennedyi*), a lily with large orange-chrome petals and contrasting purple anthers. When it comes out in force on the gravelly mesas and rocky hills, the Mohave aster (*Aster abatus*), with broad lilac-colored flowers on tall, graceful stems, presents an equally striking spectacle. In the desert's interior we see great stretches covered with carpets of short-statured, royal-purple lupines (*Lupinus odoratus*), or fields stippled lemon and green with countless stalks of caulanthus (*C. inflatus*), the squaw's cabbage of the Indians and the pioneers.

If I were asked to name the most commonly found and showy annual wild flowers of our California deserts, I would list the following: the yellow desert sunflower (*Garaea canescens*), different species of phacelia such a *P. crenulata* and *P. distans,* lupines (*L. odorata, L. arizonica*), gold dollars, sometimes called desert marigold (*Baileya radiata pleniradiata*), malocothrix or desert dandelion (*Malacothrix glabrata, Nama demissum*), several kinds of Gilia (*G. latifolia* and *G. aurea*), evening primroses (*Oenothera deltoides, O. brevipes*), Chaenactis (*Chaenactis fremontii*), and sand verbena (*Abronia villosa*). All produce mass color effects and grow best on loose sand or gravelly soils of the washes, mesas, and bajadas, and in the disturbed soil of roadsides.

On the Colorado Desert the best shows of color are made by the pink sand verbenas, golden encelias (*Geraea canescens*), great white evening primroses (*Oenothera deltoides*), gilias, yellow malocothrix, coreopsis, and blazing stars, as well as several kinds of blue lupines. The tips of the stout stems of the dying evening primroses of the dunes meet to form curious "baskets" or "bird cages" which long remain as strange decorations on the sun-drenched sands. This habit of basket formation, as yet unexplained, is shared by a number of other desert plants.

Volcanic soils and those of the flats surrounding many of the dry-type dry lakes seem unusually well suited to the needs of many kinds of wild buckwheats and chorizanthes, and among the spectacular sights of early summer are the colorful stretches of blossoming plants. As they come to maturity, the stems turn a warm chestnut red, and frequently not only the dry-lake margins but whole valley floors and their bordering detrital fans glow with ruddy color.

Careful estimates based on check lists reveal the fact that the California deserts support no less than seven hundred species of flowering plants. What a contrast is this to the monotonous and meager flora of the Old World deserts! Because of the uniformity of land surface and the lack of varied environment there, the few genera and species of plants are distributed with little interruption from the Sahara's far western limits to the mid-region of Turkestan.

The flora of much of the United States and Canada has many features in common with that of Europe and Asia, and this fact is taken as almost certain evidence of the former existence of a land bridge between Eurasia and North America. It is indeed possible that from Europe and Asia the ancestors of a good proportion of our northern flora were acquired. The botanists tell us that the deserts of North America have derived their plant genera from a very different source. The genera so common in the north are here replaced by such odd, xerophilous plants as the yuccas, agaves, ocotillos, and cacti, all plants of strictly American distribution that were probably first developed on the great arid Sonoran plateau of Mexico. It was near the end of the glacial epoch and the beginning of the development of arid conditions in California that these plants of the Mexican realm pushed northward and gave us this most unique flora. The deserts of southern Arizona and of the Salton Sea area show this invasion of the Mexican element much more strongly than the deserts of the Great Basin region.

Dr. Philip Munz lists at least 48 plants of the Colorado Desert as endemics, i.e., plants of specific and subspecific rank that are confined to a particular area and found nowhere else. Writing of endemism of the Mohave Desert, Dr. Munz says: "Perhaps almost one-fourth of the species are confined within its borders or extend only into immediately adjacent areas." About one-half of the plant species are common to both deserts.

It is now known that many desert plants, among them the hardy desert shrubs, are great drinkers and almost reckless spenders of water when they can get it. In fact, in many cases they appear to be more improvident with their water supply than plants of humid regions. In general it may be said that the chief distinction between desert plants and those of moister lands lies not, as we so often are led to believe, in their ability to get along with scant amounts of water but in their power to endure long-continued wilting and to recover from it unharmed when the rains come again. Creosote bushes near Bagdad on the Mohave Desert stood through the long drought of 1909–12 when for 32 months not a drop of precipitation was recorded and the interval between effective rains was still longer. They came to the end of the dry period with scarcely a leaf left—as miserable a lot of plants as one ever saw. How they ever became green again is little short of a mystery.

Desert plants commonly exhibit certain peculiar structural characters such as thorns and leathery leaves which are protected against evaporation by hairs, resiny coats, reduced surface, and sunken stomata. Such adaptations were long thought to be a reaction to the hot, dry atmosphere and the meager water supply at the root. When plant physiologists observed that plants of bogs and salt marshes show these same modifications it was concluded that, though the roots were planted in wet earth, they suffered from lack of water even as the desert plants did. These marsh plants, they said, were subjected to "physiological drought"—i.e., water was "considered not readily available to the plant on account of the high osmotic pressure of salt solutions, bad aeration in marshes, and bog toxins." But this explanation, they soon discovered, was not adequate. Recent studies carried on by Dr. Kurt Mothes of Germany point to the possibility that both desert and marsh and bog plants produce their similar, peculiar structures because of the lack of nitrogen in the soil.

Many desert annuals have ways to thwart germination of seeds when only small amounts of rain fall. Their seeds are coated or contain so-called growth inhibitors which prevent sprouting unless thoroughly washed away by rains in amount sufficient to enable the young plant to make a good start.

For those seeking an easy means of identifying the desert flowers, trees, and shrubs, I have made drawings of the commoner species. Unfortunately, many of the plants have had no common or English names assigned to them and we have to be content with the scientific nomen. Unless otherwise stated, all the illustrations show the plants reduced to one-half natural size. For the identification of plants not shown here, the reader is referred to the author's *Desert Wild Flowers, A Manual of the Flowering Plants of California,* by Dr. W. L. Jepson, and *A California Flora,* by Dr. Philip A. Munz and Dr. David D. Keck.

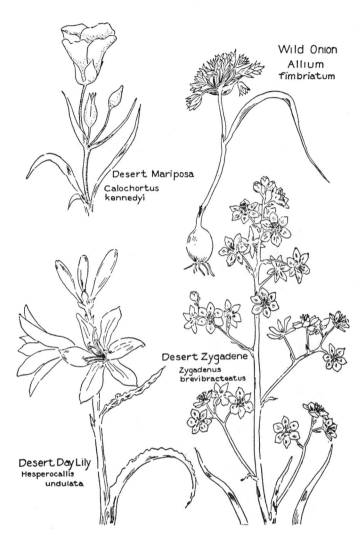

Wild Onion
Allium
fimbriatum

Desert Mariposa
Calochortus
kennedyi

Desert Zygadene
Zygadenus
brevibracteatus

Desert Day Lily
Hesperocallis
undulata

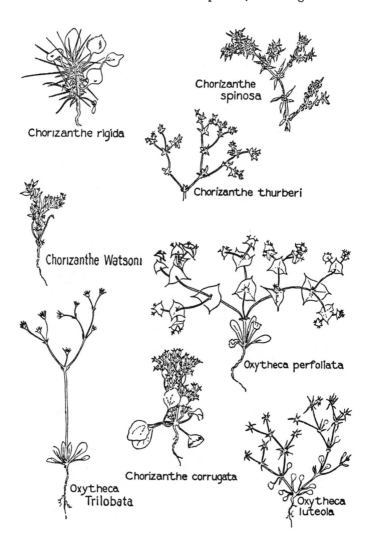

Chorizanthe rigida

Chorizanthe
spinosa

Chorizanthe thurberi

Chorizanthe Watsoni

Oxytheca perfoliata

Oxytheca
Trilobata

Chorizanthe corrugata

Oxytheca
luteola

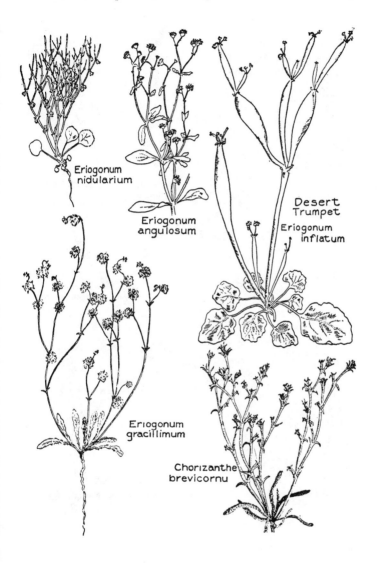

Eriogonum
nidularium

Eriogonum
angulosum

Desert
Trumpet
Eriogonum
inflatum

Eriogonum
gracillimum

Chorizanthe
brevicornu

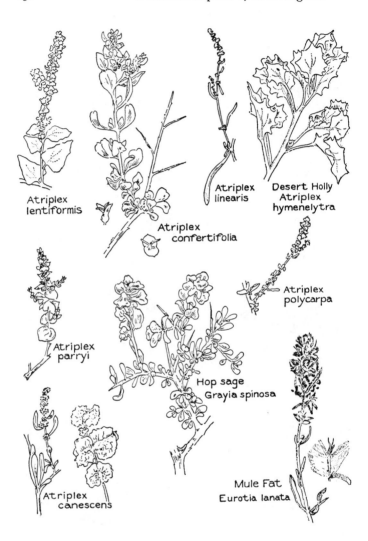

Atriplex
lentiformis

Atriplex
confertifolia

Atriplex
linearis

Desert Holly
Atriplex
hymenelytra

Atriplex
polycarpa

Atriplex
parryi

Hop sage
Grayia spinosa

Atriplex
canescens

Mule Fat
Eurotia lanata

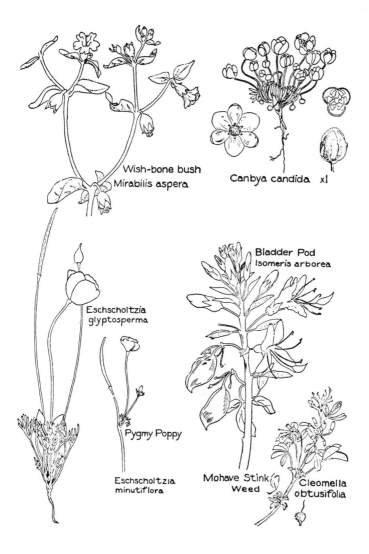

Wish-bone bush
Mirabilis aspera

Canbya candida x1

Bladder Pod
Isomeris arborea

Eschscholtzia
glyptosperma

Pygmy Poppy

Eschscholtzia
minutiflora

Mohave Stink
Weed

Cleomella
obtusifolia

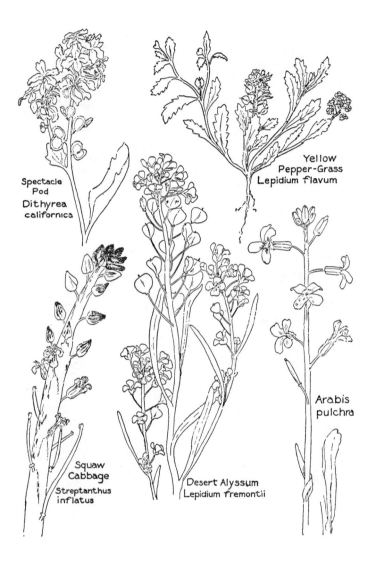

Spectacle
Pod
Dithyrea
californica

Yellow
Pepper-Grass
Lepidium flavum

Squaw
Cabbage
Streptanthus
inflatus

Desert Alyssum
Lepidium fremontii

Arabis
pulchra

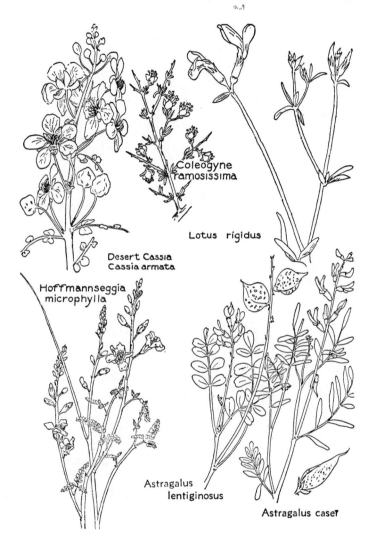

Coleogyne
ramosissima

Lotus rigidus

Desert Cassia
Cassia armata

Hoffmannseggia
microphylla

Astragalus
lentiginosus

Astragalus casei

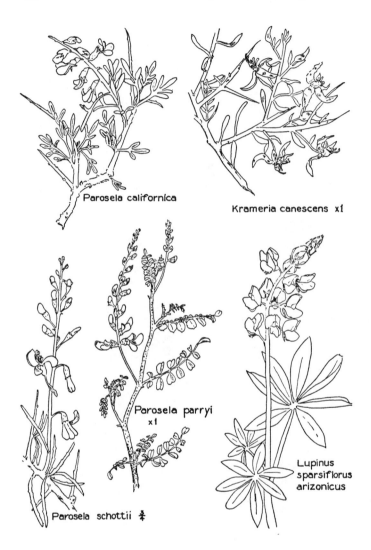

Parosela californica

Krameria canescens x1

Parosela parryi
x1

Parosela schottii ⚥

Lupinus
sparsiflorus
arizonicus

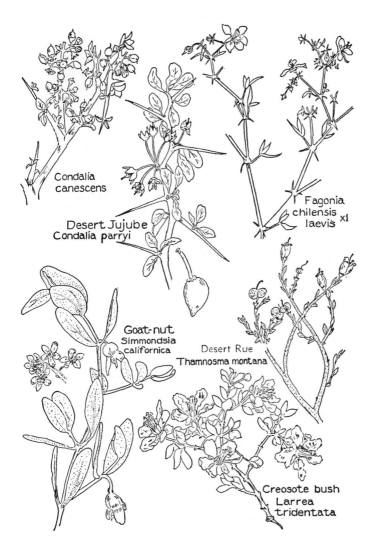

Condalia
canescens

Desert Jujube
Condalía parryi

Fagonia
chilensis
laevis x1

Goat-nut
Simmondsia
californica

Desert Rue
Thamnosma montana

Creosote bush
Larrea
tridentata

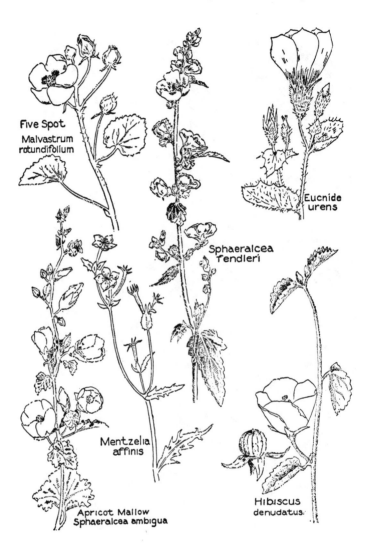

Five Spot
Malvastrum
rotundifolium

Eucnide
urens

Sphaeralcea
Tendleri

Mentzelia
affinis

Apricot Mallow
Sphaeralcea ambigua

Hibiscus
denudatus

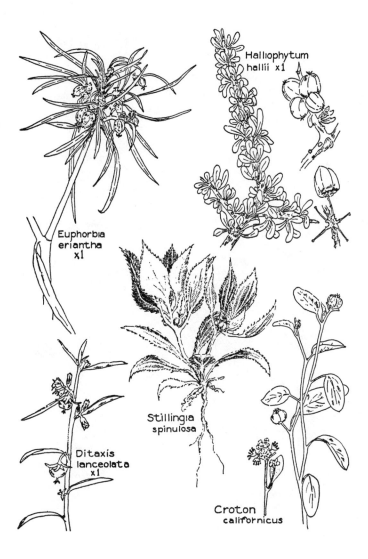

Halliophytum
hallii x1

Euphorbia
eriantha
x1

Stillingia
spinulosa

Ditaxis
lanceolata
x1

Croton
californicus

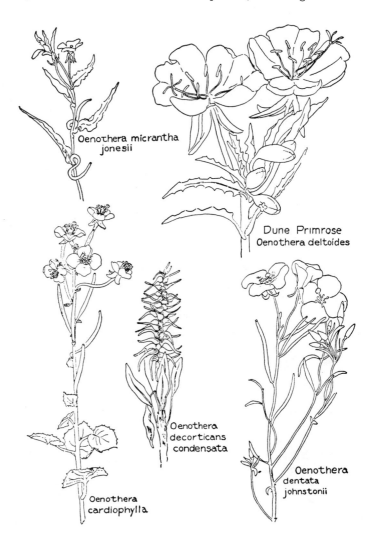

Oenothera micrantha
jonesii

Dune Primrose
Oenothera deltoides

Oenothera
decorticans
condensata

Oenothera
cardiophylla

Oenothera
dentata
johnstonii

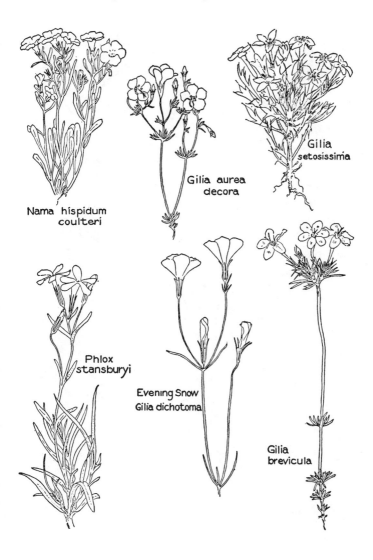

Nama hispidum
coulteri

Gilia aurea
decora

Gilia
setosissima

Phlox
stansburyi

Evening Snow
Gilia dichotoma

Gilia
brevicula

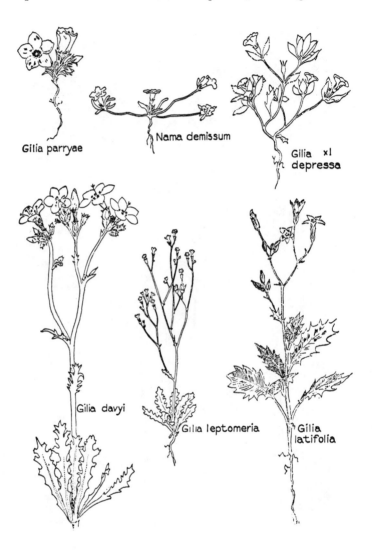

Gilia parryae

Nama demissum

Gilia depressa ×1

Gilia davyi

Gilia leptomeria

Gilia latifolia

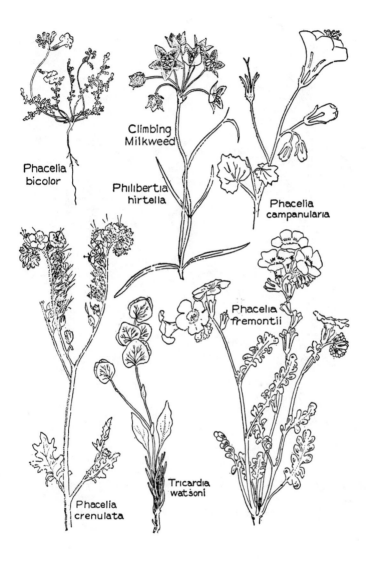

Phacelia
bicolor

Climbing
Milkweed

Philibertia
hirtella

Phacelia
campanularia

Phacelia
fremontii

Phacelia
crenulata

Tricardia
watsoni

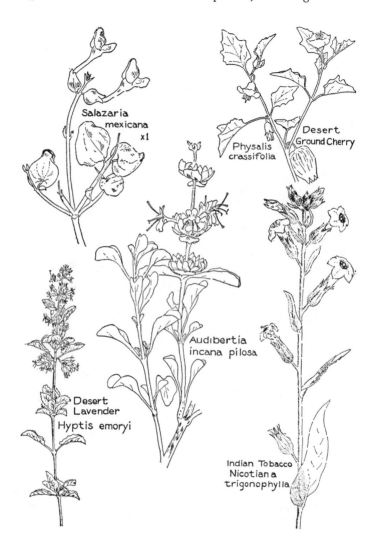

Salazaria
mexicana
x1

Physalis
crassifolia

Desert
Ground Cherry

Audibertia
incana pilosa

Desert
Lavender
Hyptis emoryi

Indian Tobacco
Nicotiana
trigonophylla

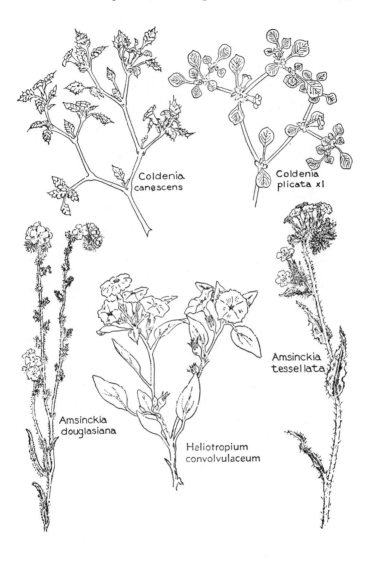

Coldenia canescens

Coldenia plicata xl

Amsinckia tessellata

Amsinckia douglasiana

Heliotropium convolvulaceum

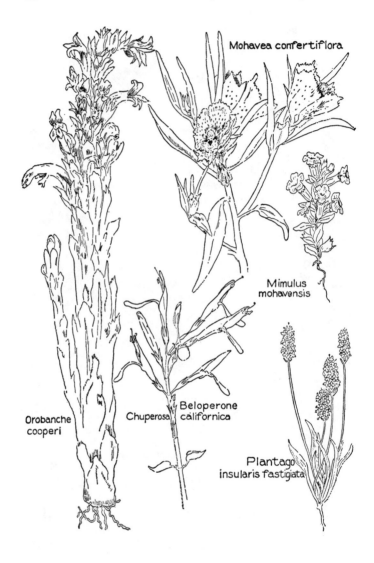

Mohavea confertiflora

Mimulus
mohavensis

Orobanche
cooperi

Chuperosa / Beloperone
californica

Plantago
insularis fastigiata

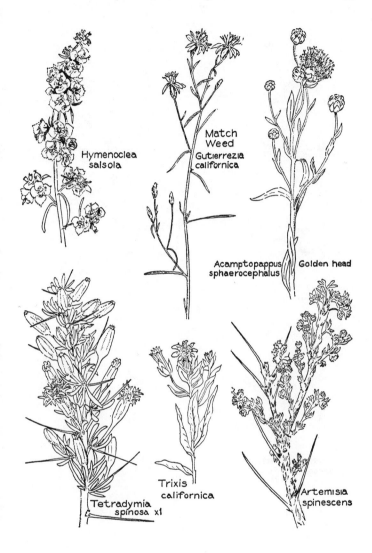

Hymenoclea
salsola

Match
Weed
Gutierrezia
californica

Acamptopappus
sphaerocephalus

Golden head

Tetradymia
spinosa x1

Trixis
californica

Artemisia
spinescens

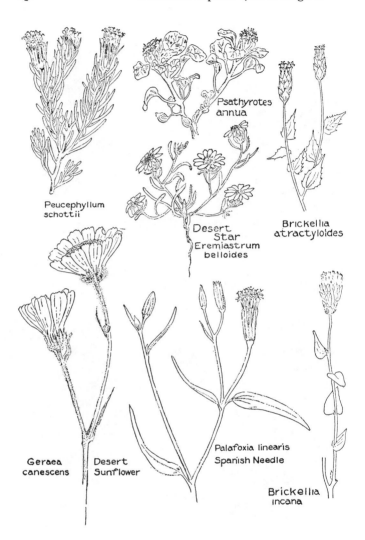

Peucephyllum
schottii

Psathyrotes
annua

Desert
Star
Eremiastrum
belloides

Brickellia
atractyloides

Geraea
canescens

Desert
Sunflower

Palafoxia linearis
Spanish Needle

Brickellia
incana

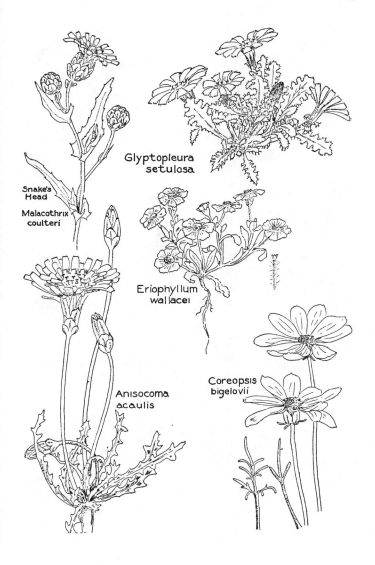

Glyptopleura
setulosa

Snake's
Head

Malacothrix
coulteri

Eriophyllum
wallacei

Anisocoma
acaulis

Coreopsis
bigelovii

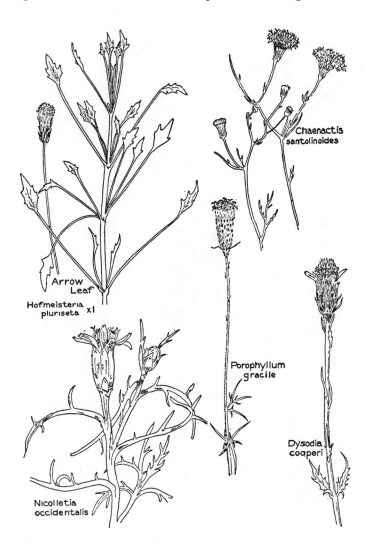

Chaenactis
santolinoides

Arrow
Leaf
Hofmeisteria x1
pluriseta

Porophyllum
gracile

Dysodia
coaperi

Nicolletia
occidentalis

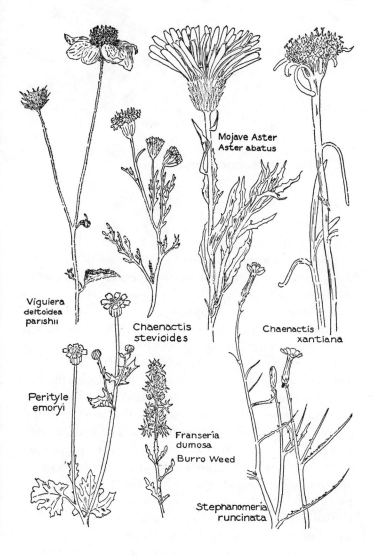

Mojave Aster
Aster abatus

Viguiera
deltoidea
parishii

Chaenactis
stevioides

Chaenactis
xantiana

Perityle
emoryi

Franseria
dumosa
Burro Weed

Stephanomeria
runcinata

12. Fungi, Ferns, and Grasses

Deserts, with their great paucity of soil humus and scanty rainfall, are seldom thought of as the home of fungi, but many specialized forms have adapted themselves to the severe conditions and from time to time show up in great abundance. When the rains dampen the soil they are able to perfect their growth in a remarkably short time. There are evidently more animal droppings and bits of decaying vegetation beneath the soil than one would suspect.

Shortly after rains and perhaps for some time afterward we see, springing up along roadsides and along the borders of the dry streamways, great numbers of that large, beautiful, glaring-white puffball, *Podaxis farlowii*. The bulbous, club-shaped tops, covered with elongated, rectangular scales, often stand four or five inches above the ground. The scales gradually come off, leaving old specimens, which persist sometimes for months, smooth and brown. A very similar if not identical puffball is said to be found in the arid wastes of the Sahara and some of the other Old World deserts.

Gyrophragmium delelei, another conspicuous fungus, is much less common, but occasionally it pushes up in great numbers through the sands of washes. The rounded, leathery, spore-bearing sac or pileus, almost the size of one's fist, looks outwardly like a puffball but when examined is seen to have gills like a mushroom, and on these the spores are borne. Probably this is the same as a Mediterranean species of like appearance.

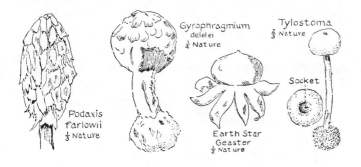

Podaxis farlowii ⅓ Nature

Gyrophragmium delelei ¼ Nature

Earth Star Geaster ½ Nature

Tylostoma ⅔ Nature

Socket

The tylostomas are small, tall-stalked puffballs with a peculiar socket at the base of the peridium into which the long stipe is inserted. A small, buttonlike, basal disk or bulb, consisting of the mycelia and intermingled sand grains, generally comes up when the plant is pulled from the sand. *Tylostoma campestre* is the common species.

Some of the earth stars (*Geaster*) are always turning up in unexpected places, especially in the dry piñon-juniper woodlands. These little globular puffballs have coverings which are distinctly two-layered. The outer layer splits into spreading, star-shaped segments, while the inner layer remains intact except for a little chimneylike pore through which the black powdery spores come out.

Quite a number of rusts occur on plants of the desert area. These fungi depend for their existence entirely upon the living cells of the plants on which they are found as continuous parasites. Some of them have alternate hosts, living during one part of their existence on one species of plant and during another on another plant. Some alternate hosts are as different as the oak and a grass. Some of the common and interesting ones are mentioned in connection with their plant hosts. (See pages 162, 163.)

Many of the dull-hued rocks of arid regions are ornamented with the bright colors of incrusting lichens. An entirely new and engaging pleasure may be derived from a study and collection of the various forms.

The largest and finest splashes of vivid color occur on the north and northeast faces of black lava blocks of the Mohave region. Here, receiving the least exposure to the drying winds, the red, rock-wall lichen (*Caloplaca murorum*) paints the rock surface a striking reddish-brown, and *Acarospora chlorophana* spreads its coat of brilliant yellowish-green. With them may be growing *Lecanora saxicola,* another dainty, rock-hugging form of blue-gray hue.

Among the next most conspicuous lichens are *Acarospora epilutescens* (silver gray) and *Candelariella vitellina* (a deep, golden yellow), the last particularly beautiful when growing with other colorful species. Some of the black lichens occupy the sides of rocks in the most exposed situations, seeming to mind neither scorching sun nor desiccating winds.

Though in summer the withered plants apparently are as dry as the rock surfaces themselves, they are never without moisture. In winter they often get dampness directly from the rains that fall upon them, but in summer, said Dr. Albert Herre, "it is highly probable that the great diurnal drop in temperature which comes in all arid regions with the advent of darkness is likewise accompanied by a deposition of moisture or at least an increase in water content of desert lichens."

"When one considers," Dr. Herre further said, "that the temperature drops 30 to 35 degrees F. every night during summer months, it is apparent that without any increase in the actual amount of water present there is a great increase in the percentage of moisture, and it is believed by some of us that the lichens are able to take advantage of this relative increase and absorb enough moisture to maintain their vitality during the long, hot, dry season.

"That desert conditions are, in the main, unfavorable to the growth of lichens as a whole is shown by the limited number of genera and species represented, while a considerable number of those found are able to maintain themselves only in the most favorable spots, such as under overhanging rocks on the north side of cliffs within crevices. But that some species are perfectly at home in the midst of the most adverse desert conditions of excessive light and dryness is shown by the fact that almost everywhere the rocks are just as thickly covered with lichens as in other regions of greater humidity and less sunshine. The desert does not lack in number of individuals, but in number of species of lichens able to adapt themselves to its conditions."

It appears reasonable to believe that the presence of desert varnish is sometimes due to organic agencies such as the growth and disintegration of lichens. Dr. J. D. Loudermilk, who had examined many of the dark, "varnished" rock areas of the flat mesas of the Mohave Desert, noticed that they frequently occur as well-defined, circular patches in areas of similar but uncoated rocks. Investigation showed that the dark rock surfaces were in many instances covered with colonies of small, almost microscopic, incrusting lichens. It is thought that the acids secreted by the lichens corrode the outer layers of the rocks and that the dissolved minerals, after having been taken up by the plants, are again deposited as oxides on the rock surfaces after the death of the lichens.

We are so accustomed to associate ferns with regions of dampness that it may be a surprise to many to know that at least twelve species belonging to three different genera are found in the territory under consideration. Subjected almost constantly to the drying winds, they have uniquely modified not only their structure but also their life histories in order to protect themselves from excessive transpiration and the caprices of an arid climate. The fronds are unusually small and thick and the pinnae multiplied and much divided. Some desert ferns have viscid coatings of wax; others are densely woolly or are clad in an armor of overlapping scales or hair which serves both as a protection and as a moisture-retaining covering.

These ferns must make their entire growth in the winter and spring season of rain and be ready to spend the dry summer days in dormancy. "But these rains," as the late S. B. Parish said, "are small in amount at any one time, they are uncertain, and the moisture is liable to be speedily evaporated by drying winds. Their fronds, therefore, unfold at once as soon as moistened by the first showers and resume life at the point where they dropped its functions, perhaps months ago. How long this active life may continue depends wholly upon the meteorological conditions. So long as moisture is attainable there is no cessation; but as soon as it fails, active life is suspended. In this condition the fern appears dead; the frond is dry and crumbles in the fingers; the stipe and rhizome are brittle and break up in handling. These resting fronds assume various forms. Many curl up into more or less compact balls, exposing to the air the back of the frond, which is the most heavily protected."

The golden-back fern (*Pityrogramma triangularis*) as well as the coffee fern (*Pellaea andromadaefolia*) and the bird's foot (*Pellaea mucronata*), so common in the southern California foothills, reach the desert borders but are not generally found far to the eastward. It is the cloak ferns of the genus *Notholaena* and *Cheilanthes*, with the coverings of woolly hairs, that are most successful in the more arid, interior deserts. Four species of cloak ferns occur in the shelter of rocks, Parry's cloak fern (*N. parryi*) being the most widespread. This has pinnae so densely hairy that they look like pellets of wool. Jones's cloak fern (*N. jonesii*), with its few scattered, leathery pinnae, is extensive in distribution by very rare. The sinuate cloak fern (*N. sinuata*) is known in California only from the Providence Mountains and Clark Mountain. Eastward it is known from Arizona and Mexico.

The lip ferns, so called because of the ·in-rolling of the

edges of the sori, are represented by the viscid lip fern (*Chei-lanthes viscida*) with its remarkably sticky herbage (first collected by Dr. C. C. Parry and Mr. J. G. Lemmon, pioneer botanical explorers, at Whitewater), and *C. feei* of the Providence Mountains with dense, close hair on the undersurface of the fronds. Coville's lip fern (*C. covillei*) is a fine little plant with closely set, beady end-segments, found plentifully not only in the desert mountains but also in some of the foothills nearer the coast.

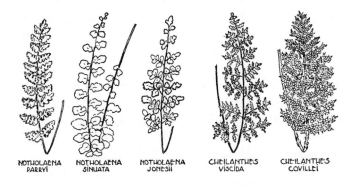

NOTHOLAENA PARRYI   NOTHOLAENA SINUATA   NOTHOLAENA JONESII   CHEILANTHES VISCIDA   CHEILANTHES COVILLEI

Dry desert canyons would seem to hold little promise of our finding the delicate, water-loving maidenhair ferns, but in damp recesses of rocky grottoes or under shelving banks in the box canyons we sometimes come upon them; both are coastal species which have found footing in the deserts, or perhaps they are holdovers from a time when the deserts enjoyed a moister climate.

Vying with the ferns in meeting the conditions of almost perennial drought are the little-noticed, mosslike selaginellas. In the canyons and on the hillsides of the mountains near Palm Springs, and southward along the Colorado Desert's western border, thence eastward to the Chuckawalla Mountains, also to Arizona and lower California, the arid selaginella (*Selaginella eremophila*), with strong, flattened, bright-green branches which root on the underside, grows in

large cushions at the foot of rocks, often mingling with the
ascending branches of the coastal selaginella (*S. bigelovii*).
Differing in foliage characters from all other Pacific Coast
species is *S. leucobryoides,* found in the Panamint and Providence mountains. The most striking of its characteristics are
"the extremely short, pure white, but opaque, setae of the
leaves and the condensed, rosette-like arrangement of the very
short branches" (Maxon).

No fewer than thirty-three kinds of grasses are listed from
the California deserts. The dominant, conspicuous species
are of the perennial bunch type. Galleta (pronounced locally
Guy-ee-et'-ta) grass (*Hilaria rigida*), an erect grass about a
foot high, is plentiful in many of the basins of both deserts.
Its stiffish, felty-haired stems are rich in nourishment for
grazing animals, and the cowmen always count it a stroke of
good luck when they find it growing near enough to water
holes and springs to make it available for feed. Inspection of
the stem bases soon reveals large bulbous galls about an inch
in diameter which appear like little fat ears of popcorn.
These deformities, the interiors of which are hard as wood,
are caused by a large eurytomid wasp (*Harmolita*), whose
larvae develop within the tissues. A chance to see good stands
of galleta grass is offered the traveler in West Cronese Valley
on the road between Barstow and Las Vegas. In the most arid
parts of its range the stems become very large and hard and
when eaten by cattle may puncture the digestive tube. In the
high deserts of Inyo County and the Great Basin is another
galleta grass (*Hilaria jamesii*) with smooth, hairless stems. Indian rice (*Oryzopsis hymenoides*) is frequent in porous soils,
particularly on blown sand. The diffuse panicles bear hosts
of large, plump seeds which are much relished by grazing
animals. It is one of our most beautiful grasses and among
our few sand-binding species. It was of great importance to
the Indians as a food source. A very common and very handsome bunch grass of the high desert valleys is the desert

needle grass (*Stipa speciosa*). It grows about a foot high and is plentiful among the junipers. Good open stands may be seen to advantage by the traveler between Cajon summit and Victorville. The blackened tufts of dead specimens are often very conspicuous.

The grass called red bromus (*Bromus ruber*), an import from southern Europe, is now widespread on our deserts, often far away from cultivated areas. In many places it has displaced the native grasses.

After spring rains the little frost grass (*Triodia pulchella*) comes up in enormous quantities and, true to its common name, makes the desert where it grows appear as if covered with frost. The little clumps are often three or four inches across. The short, slender stems of *Triodia pulchella* have a peculiar way of bending over and taking root again. Another triodia (*T. mutica*), more erect and with flower panicles slender, is found in the Eagle and Chuckawalla mountains. About the desert springs and along some of the tiny streams of the canyons occurs the common reed (*Phragmites communis*), with stems four or five feet high or sometimes higher. It is often called carrizo (Spanish *carrizal,* reed grass). In damp, alkaline soils, salt grass (*Distichlis spicata*) is often very abundant and is about the only plant that takes root there. It saved the life of many a hungry mule and ox in the days of pioneer travel.

There are two cattails (*Typha*) found about subalkaline desert springs and streams. The more common slender-stemmed cattail (*T. angustifolia*) is usually rather low, with the leaves very narrow. The long spike has the staminate (male) and pistillate (female) portions usually unseparated. The tall, stout broad-leafed cattail (*T. latifolia*) has the staminate and pistillate parts of the dark brown fruiting spike usually separated by a small interval.

13. Shrubs

The desert is surprisingly rich in the number of its woody herbs and shrubs, the general coloration of which is gray-green. To their dry, gray barks and hair-covered leaves is due the monotonous aspect of much of the arid Southwest. Only along or near moist streamways and washes or in the semisheltered canyons of the higher mountains do the shrubs attain sizable proportions. In the broad, practically water-less valleys, where arid conditions are intensified, most of them grow no higher than a man's knee. The further one penetrates northeastward into the desert's interior the more stunted the shrubs become. The number of species also rap-idly dwindles until we encounter, in some of the broad basins of the eastern Mohave Desert, great areas whose only con-spicuous plants are those great water-conservers, the creosote bush and the burroweed. In parts of Panamint Valley's parched floor even the burroweed cannot withstand the ter-rific struggle, and creosote alone braves the hot winds and glaring light of the summer sun. Because they are well spaced and equally exposed to light from all sides, the characteristic form of most desert shrubs is globular or hemispherical. All unsheltered desert perennials are subject to strong winds, and this results in a low, squat form which is a distinct advantage to them. The extensive root systems, built primarily for the absorption of moisture, serve as extraordinarily trusty anchors in times of stress.

The physical texture and chemical composition of the rocks of which mountains are built influences not only the type of flora but also the altitude to which the desert plants ascend the slopes. Mountains of granite and limestone favor the retention of moisture in the surface rocks much better than mountains of coarse-textured rhyolite and lavas. The Granite Mountains north of Amboy, the New York Mountains, the Old Woman Mountains, and Clark Mountain for this reason support a good mantle of brush far down their slopes, whereas other neighboring mountains of approximately the same altitude but made of volcanic rock are barren, even at their summits, of all but the hardiest desert shrubs.

In the upland belts of junipers and tree yuccas the predominant shrubs are the tetradymias, rabbit brushes, and senecios. Many of these come into flower late in the season, making the areas gay with shades of yellow. In the late spring, when the blue sage (*Salvia carnosa pilosa* = *S. Dorrii*) bursts into bloom, many of the high mesas of the Mohave are masses of brilliant sky blue.

Below the zone of tree yuccas, the creosote bush (*Larrea divaricata*) takes possession. About the only place it does not grow is in the soils poisoned by sulphates or in the flat, salt-incrusted lake beds. Often it occurs in uncountable numbers and in almost pure stands, giving a lovely, brownish-green aspect to the floors of the spacious basins of the Mohave region. The seeds are slow to germinate and it takes peculiar combinations of heat and moisture to start the young plant. Except in spots, young bushes are certainly not plentiful. Most of the large shrubs appear to be very old. It is the lack of soil water which probably accounts for the amazingly regular spacing of the plants. The brown or green balls, each of them about the size of a small walnut, which appear on the stems, are made by a small fly, the creosote gall-midge (*Asphondylia auripila*). Though outwardly covered by hundreds of soft, dwarfed leaves, the interiors of the galls are hard and woody, and in this portion the larvae develop.

Associated with the creosote bush, especially in the higher elevations of the Mohave Desert, is the spiny hop sage (*Grayia spinosa*), the winged fruits of which are often tinged with rich shades of pink and maroon. There too are found the scraggly salazaria, with its bladderlike pods, and the very twiggy coleogyne. The last often occurs in such pure stands on the high alluvial fans that the whole area of dominance is colored a military blue-gray.

Species of ephedra or Mexican tea occur in similar situations. The ephedras have been given many common names: Mormon tea, teamster's tea, desert tea, Brigham tea, squaw tea, and canatello are just a few of the names in common use among the desert folk, who make a beverage of it by boiling a handful of the stems for a few minutes in water. All the ephedras have long-jointed, fluted stems which bear minute, scalelike leaves at the nodes. The male plants are showy in spring and bear, in abundance, catkins with prominent, protruding yellow stamens of remarkable beauty. The California ephedra (*Ephedra californica*), with yellowish-green stems and leaf scales arranged in threes, is the commonest one. The spindle-shaped swellings on the stems are caused by a tiny, slender fly, the fusiform gall-fly (*Lasioptera ephedrae*), belonging to the same family of gall-makers (*Cecidomyiidae*) as the creosote gall-midge.

Particularly common on the Mohave Desert is the gray-green Nevada ephedra (*E. nevadensis*). *Ephedra viridis*, with its numerous yellow-green branches occurring in broomlike clusters, is a very handsome plant of the desert mountains. It makes the richest-flavored tea of any the species.

The shrubby paroselas, sometimes called daleas, call attention to themselves by their brilliant royal-purple, pealike flowers. Most of them have herbage that is highly glandular, and they give off, when crushed, an agreeable spicy odor. At least one species (*Parosela emoryi*) yielded a yellow dye to the Indians. The center of distribution of the paroselas is Mexico, where more than 120 species are known.

The two species of krameria (*Krameria parvifolia* and *canescens*) are low, thorny shrubs, conspicuous in the vernal season because of their lovely wine-colored flowers and later because of their many odd, spine-tipped fruits. The kramerias derive most of their nourishment parasitically with the aid of pecular root-pads which rest like saddles on the roots of other plants.

With gray-green stems, woefully naked for eleven months of the year, the desert cassias suddenly become in late April the showiest plants of the washes and mesas. Such a wealth of yellow flowers is a rare sight among desert shrubs. *Cassia armata* is the common species.

Franseria or white burroweed (*Franseria dumosa*) is probably the second most abundant shrub of our Southwestern deserts. It is a low, rounded bush of grayish hue generally found filling in gaps between the rather orderly spaced creosote bushes. It is a most excellent browsing plant, four or five large bushes making a day's food for a burro. I cannot imagine why the animals like the bitter stuff.

In the Chuckawalla Mountains, along the rocky edges of sand washes, grows here and there the rare holly-leaved franseria (*Franseria ilicifolia*). After rains some of the large spiny leaves may be green but many are always dead, paper-dry, and fawn- to gray-colored. The prickly burrs may be a half-inch in diameter.

Along the clayey banks of washes at low elevations one is quite likely to see the goat-nut (*Simmondsia californica*), an erect, very drought-resistant shrub about three or four feet high, possessing ovoid, gray-green leaves, which are remarkably leathery and thick. It bears a nut which rodents evidently consider not at all bad eating, for in autumn we often run across stores of the nuts which have been gathered and hidden under rocks by mice and little antelope chipmunks. Cattle, when driven by hunger, crop the leaves closely.

If among the creosote bushes you find a very spiny shrub on which are many little red or green, tomatolike fruits, you may be certain you have found one of the lyciums or wolf bushes. The tubular flowers, colored white, pale purple, or lavender, are borne in abundance among the fascicles of small leathery or somewhat fleshy leaves. *Lycium pallidum,* of the Mohave Desert, with lavender to yellow, short, trumpet-shaped flowers, is the most decorative. The quail are fond of the juicy red fruits, which at times may furnish their sole water supply. *Lycium cooperi,* named after Dr. J. G. Cooper who collected plants on the eastern Mohave Desert in the 1860's, is generally found in colonies, most frequently in gravelly soils. Its stout, erect, blackish stems, about three feet tall, bear numerous leaves, densely crowded and greenish-white flowers. The fruit is also greenish-white.

Several shrubby herbaceous perennials are conspicuous in the sand washes of the Mohave Desert. Among them are the fine-stemmed match weeds (*Gutierrezia*), which we prize above all other plants as tinder for our fires, the gritty-leaved sandpaper bush (*Petalonyx thurberi*), and several of the resin-filled ericamerias. The ashy-green *Ericameria paniculata* is particularly a prominent wash plant of the northern Mohave Desert. It is associated with senecio (*S. douglasii*) and scale-broom (*Lepidospartum squamatum*), and after the summer rains they all burst into yellow bloom, attracting great numbers of insects. The refreshing bright green herbage of the foul-odored hymenoclea (*Hymenoclea salsola*) completes the pleasing picture. Its strong roots penetrate deep to the moist wash-sands and it manages to stay green during most of the year. A smut fungus (*Puccinia splendens*) often causes the stems to break open and turn black.

Along dry streamways of the Colorado Desert there are several shrubs particularly common. One of these is the bladder-pod (*Isomeris arborea*). It blooms throughout the year and its yellow blossoms often lend the only bits of bright color to the otherwise drab scene. Though the foliage is foul-scented, we admire the plant for the delicate appearance of its flowers and its pendant, inflated fruits. The desert lavender (*Hyptis emoryi*), another large, wash-inhabiting shrub with wand-like branches, compels our notice because of its almost constant show of woolly, blue-gray masses of minute, mintlike flowers. The plant is not tolerant of heavy frosts and is for this reason largely confined to the southern desert. It is a great bee plant and often the special nesting site of the plumbeous gnatcatcher and the verdin. The peculiar blackish growths on the woody parts of the stems are due to a rust fungus (*Puccinia distorta*). The presence of the smut is one of the chief causes of the large number of dead limbs. In the same dry streamways grows the scarlet-flowered beloperone (*Beloperone californica*), one of the earliest and most persistent bloomers of the year. Because of the color and form of its flowers, many mistake it for a bush pentstemon. Its tubular flowers are often visited by humming birds for the nectar, hence its Spanish name, "chuparosa," meaning "sucking rose." The house finches sometimes bite off the corolla tubes to get at the nectar glands and ovaries.

When we approach the dry-lake bottoms we encounter a whole new assemblage of plants—plants which must draw upon the highly alkaline soils for their moisture. Among these are cattle spinach (*Atriplex polycarpa*), sarcobatus (the true greasewood), suaeda, succulent-jointed desert pickle-wort (*Allenrolfea occidentalis,* named after Allen Rolfe, one-time botanist at Kew Gardens, London), and several kinds of isocoma.

Along the irrigation canals and other ponded waters of the Imperial Valley are abundant growths of arrowweed, the tall-stemmed Indian hemp (*Sesbiana macrocarpa*), the spiny, deep-rooted, and difficult-to-eradicate spiny aster (*Aster spinosa*), the screw-bean mesquite, cattails, the small pink-flowered athel (*Tamarix gallica*), the bamboolike common rush (*Phragmites communis*), and salt grass. Together with such birds as the roadrunner, the verdin, the yellow-headed and red-winged blackbirds, and the Salton Sea song sparrow, and among such mammals as the muskrat and cotton rat they form a unique biotic community.

Saltbushes are plants inhabiting alkaline soils throughout all of the Western deserts. They are often tolerant of very dry soils. The most widespread Mohavean saltbush is *Atriplex confertifolia,* known as sheep-fat or spiny saltbush. The low, compact bushes are not wholly confined to alkaline areas but are generally distributed among shrubs of the broad basins of the Mohave region from the vicinity of Barstow northward. In the Salton Sink, *A. canescens* (sometimes called four-wing saltbush) is very abundant in both dry and damp soils of both deserts, and *A. lentiformis,* the quail bush, forms enormous thickets in the damp, saline soils and rich bottom-lands of the Salton Sink and the Colorado River. These shrubby plants offer to the quail, to roadrunners, desert sparrows, and other birds very adequate protection from birds of prey. The handsome, silver-leaved desert holly is one of the saltbushes that flourishes best in the hot, gravelly, alkaline hills of the Mohave Desert, but it is not at all uncommon on the Colorado Desert among the low hills to the east of the Salton Sea, thence southward into Lower California.

In those barren hills and low mountains that lie about the bases of the Santa Rosa and Laguna mountains of the Colorado Desert, in soil so rocky, dry, and alkaline that the hardiest desert shrubs grow scarcely above three spans high, colonies of the desert agave (*Agave deserti*) flourish and multiply. The whole aspect of the plant, from the rosette of thick, blue-green, spine-armed leaves to the tall, rigid scapes bearing the leathery flowers, well matches the arid environment.

On the limestone slopes of the far eastern Mohave Desert ranges (Clark, Ivanpah, Kingston) is found a very small, attractive, and rare short-leafed agave (*A. utahensis* var. *nevadensis*) with very long, slender flower stalks. It usually occurs in colonies.

On the same day that Emory and his forlorn soldiers saw their first Washingtonia palms (page 180), they came upon this agave and through thickets of it they rode for miles. "The sharp thorns terminating every leaf of this plant," said Emory, "were a great annoyance to our dismounted and weary men whose legs were now almost bare. A number of these plants were cut by the soldiers, and the body of them used as food. The day was intensely hot and the sand deep; the animals, inflated with water and rushes, gave way by scores: and, although we advanced only 16 miles, many did not arrive at camp until 10 o'clock that night. It was a feast day for the wolves which followed in packs close to our track, seizing our deserted brutes and making the air resound with their howls as they battled for the carcasses."

Of the shrubby yuccas, the Mohave yucca (*Yucca schidigera*) is the most widespread. Its stems, armed with long, yellow-green, daggerlike leaves, sometimes reach upward higher than a man's head. Its leaves furnished the Indians strong fibers for weaving and cordage and its basal central stem, when roasted in pits, was a nourishing food. Within the far eastern borders of California grows *Y. baccata,* a plant easily distinguished from our other desert yuccas by its grayish blue-green leaves and enormous fruits. Its leaves are all basal. On the high slopes of the New York Mountains and vicinity it consorts with junipers, Mohave yuccas, tree yuccas, and piñons.

The two species of nolina are often mistaken for some of the shrubby yuccas. The Parry nolina (*Nolina parryae*) is a very showy species when in flower and particularly noticed in May and June by visitors to the north side of the eastern

San Bernardino Mountains and to Joshua Tree National
Monument, where it occurs in many places up among the
rocks of the mountainsides. The much smaller Bigelow's
nolina (*N. bigelovii*) is also found in the Monument but is
mostly seen in the southern portion. The leaves of both kinds
of nolina are flexible, not rigid as in yuccas, and the flowers
are smaller as are also the seed vessels. The seeds of nolina
are small and round whereas those of the yuccas are flat. Nolina seeds when eaten are said to be poisonous to human beings.

About once a year I receive from some desert prospector
a shrub made up wholly of rigid, gray-green, sharp-pointed
stems, and with the gift comes the remark, "This is the thorn
out of which they made the crown for Christ when he was
crucified." Of course it is not, but the situation is hard to ex-
plain to the prospector. Specimens are usually collected on
alluvial bottomlands of the Colorado River, where the spiny
shrub grows in considerable abundance. *Holocantha emoryi,*
as it is known to botanists, is a near-relative of the Chinese
tree of heaven (*Ailanthus*). It is common enough in southern
Arizona but seems to have established itself in only a few
places on the deserts here (Coyote Wells, east of El Centro,
formerly also at The Hayfields, east of Mecca). The dense
clusters of nutlike fruits make good donkey feed, but the
plants are otherwise worthless to man.

One of the thorniest and most striking plants of the desert
area is the ocotillo (*Fouquieria splendens*), which, because of
its many vicious spines, is often erroneously brigaded with
the cacti. Ascending from a stout basal stem, the many long,
canelike, thorn-armed branches reach upward, sometimes to
a height of twenty feet. The time of flowering is late April,
but rains at unusual times cause the plants to come into full
leaf and to blossom out of season. If there is a time of long
lack of rains, the leaves turn red and fall off. Ocotillo is thus
a good example of a drought-deciduous shrub. The panicles

of scarlet, tubular flowers atop the graceful stems make the desert hills and bajadas aflame with color. Plants bearing a hundred or more ascending branches, each bearing its brilliant flowers, are not at all uncommon.

The true sagebrush (*Artemisia tridentata*), bearing spatula-shaped leaves of gray-green color, occupies only a few high-altitude areas where the rainfall is fairly well distributed throughout the year. Though it is familiar enough to residents of Utah and Nevada, it is not so well known among desert people in California. To many campers the sweet-scented smoke floating upward from sagebrush campfires is rivaled as a provoker of pleasant memories only by the aromatic smoke of burning creosote twigs.

The sagebrush is often a long-lived shrub. Studies made by tree-ring students indicate an age of over two hundred years for certain plants growing high on the arid slopes of the Inyo Mountains. Some of the large ephedra bushes of the same area were determined to be almost as old. Because of the great resistance to decay of the outer coats of pollen grains with their very distinctive sculpturing they can assist us much in our search for the nature of flora of the past. Deep drillings in the clays and other detrital materials of several of the deserts' dry lakes have revealed pollen grains of sagebrush showing a long history of that plant in past millenniums. The science of pollen grain analysis is called palynology.

The cacti belong almost entirely to the New World. They are widely distributed over the arid Southwest but are abundant only in those places where water supplies are seasonally plentiful. Such conditions obtain in the higher desert ranges and on many of the encircling alluvial fans whose washes carry the rapid runoff of summer cloudbursts and winter rains. Loose gravels or sandy, well-drained soils seem absolutely necessary for prolific growth. The long corky-barked roots, many of them several yards long, are purposely laid close to the soil surface and are always eager to take up the water of either shallow or penetrating rains. Of very greatest interest is the fact that the cacti are our only desert plants storing water in the stems. This stored water is given up very reluctantly even during the hottest days. But the ingress of carbon dioxide, which, with water, is the chief raw material utilized by the plant in the manufacture of its food, is also checked at the same time, and this is the reason why cacti are usually such slow growers.

The cactus family is here represented by at least ten species of Opuntia, three species of the genus Cereus, four of Echinocactus, and possibly four of Mammillaria. Of these, two are wholly Colorado Desert forms, nine entirely Mohavean; the remaining ten are common to both deserts.*

The opuntias or prickly-pear cacti are divided into two groups—those with cylindrical stems (*Cylindropuntia*), and those with flattened stems (*Platyopuntia*).

Opuntias with cylindrical stems.—Darning-needle cactus (*O. ramosissima*), as its specific name implies, is a much-branched, erect shrub with slender, very woody stems. Each of the joints is about two inches long and bears long spines (1½ inches) covered with yellow sheaths. The joints during summer frequently turn reddish. It is found on both deserts eastward to Nevada and Arizona. The flowers are purplish but not showy.

Bigelow's cholla (*O. bigelovii*), sometimes called "bad cholla," is the spiniest and most vicious of all our cacti. Individual plants often congregate to form thickets on the dissected benches and alluvial fans issuing from the mouths of the large canyons. No other species presents such interesting forms or gives such fine color effects. The tracts of chollas with their blendings of greens and browns are always alluring. Because the seeds are usually sterile, propagation is ef-

---

* When the deserts are more thoroughly explored and the cacti are more carefully studied the list will doubtless be extended.

fected principally by detachment of the fleshy joints. The thickly interwoven needles are strongly barbed and once in the flesh stick with persistence and leave a painful wound. This species is seldom found on the Mohave Desert but is plentiful on the Colorado Desert.

Beaver Tail Cactus

Bigelow's Cholla

Mohave Niggerhead

Deerhorn Cactus

Deerhorn cactus (*O. echinocarpa*) is surely our commonest species. The compact crowns are widespreading and made of interwoven, loosely branched joints, three to six inches long and one inch or more thick. The spines, both long and short ones, are yellowish and covered with papery sheaths which when chewed taste like witch hazel. The flowers are yellow, sometimes tinged with red, and are not particularly pleasing. This cactus is common on both deserts eastward to Utah and Arizona. It seldom forms thickets. The handsomest specimens I have ever seen grow on the sands to the northeast of the symmetrical cinder cone directly north of Little Lake.

The spiny-fruited cholla (*O. acanthocarpa*) is an erect species somewhat resembling deerhorn cactus but of more open growth. From the few stout main stems project numerous green branches, the joints of which bear elongate tubercles armed with groups of yellow spines, each about an inch long. The flowers are yellow to reddish. This cactus is plentiful in the higher mountains of the eastern Mohave Desert.

The club-jointed opuntia (*O. parishii*) is a rarely noticed cactus, even though it possesses handsome ovate fruits. The flattened, gray-brown spines adorn the short, prostrate, club-like stems in radiating clusters. The roots are on the underside of the joints. The spreading mats, made of joints well-hidden with spines, have all the appearance of being dried up and dead. This is principally a Mohavean species found at high altitudes (4,000 to 5,000 feet). Its blossoms are said to last but an hour.

Opuntias with flat stems.—Beaver-tail or slipper-sole cactus (*O. basilaris*) is a low, spreading species having joints without spines but viciously armed with myriads of brown, prickly hairs called glochids. It is widely distributed from sea level to 8,000 feet, varying much in form and in the luxuriance of its joints, according to altitude. Its brilliant rose-purple flowers appear most handsome against the neutral gray background of flat stems. The Cahuilla Indians, after removing the hairs by rolling the parts in the sand, cook the tender fruits and succulent stems with meat and pronounce it to be an excellent dish.

Newly decomposing cactus joints, especially those of the flat-stemmed opuntias, are the feeding habitats of several kinds of insect larvae, including those of flies and beetles. Earwigs have been taken there, also. The watery necrotic tissues comprise an important ecological niche to the immature insect forms, protecting them from adverse climatic conditions, especially during the period of summer's drought and high temperatures.

Grizzly bear cactus (*O. ursina*) is a fine species with ascending joints almost completely hidden by the remarkable, long, ashy-gray or white spines (3 to 10 inches long) which bend under touch like bristles. It has been much sought by cactus fanciers, and the beds which are locally abundant on the Mohave Desert have been repeatedly raided.

Hedgehog cactus (*O. erinacea*) is somewhat similar to grizzly bear cactus in general appearance, but is has shorter joints and the brownish spines are less flexible. It is locally abundant on high gravelly or stony slopes of the Mohave Desert and eastward to Nevada, Utah, and Arizona.

The remarkable pancake cactus (*O. chlorotica*) has great, flat, orbicular joints "like pancakes" (3 to 8 inches in diameter), light green in color, and armed with many close-set groups of handsome, golden-yellow spines. The trunk is almost as spiny as the joints. This large, erect, stout-stemmed cactus is usually found singly in rocky situations on the slopes of the desert mountains.

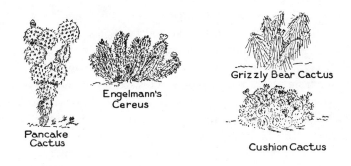

Grizzly Bear Cactus

Engelmann's Cereus

Pancake Cactus

Cushion Cactus

The Mohave opuntia (*O. mojavensis*) is a prostrate species of the bajadas and mountains of the Mohave Desert. It has large, flat, round joints (8 to 12 inches in diameter) resembling those of *O. chlorotica*. On the upper border of the joints are numerous clusters of golden spines. The stout, rigid needles, from one to one and a half inches long and borne in clusters of two to six, are white but with reddish-brown bases. The flowers are yellow, the fruits spineless.

All our cacti of the genus *Cereus* and *Echinocactus* possess globate or columnar stems bearing ridges on which the spines occur in bundles. In the genus *Cereus* the spines are borne below the summit of the ribs; in the genus *Echinocactus,* at the summit. The flowers are often brilliantly colored.

Engelmann's cereus (*C. engelmanni*), a handsome, purple-flowered species, is a rival in beauty of the regal *Opuntia basilaris*. It is common in the rocky hills and wastes throughout our Southwestern deserts up to 8,000 feet altitude. The rounded stems, each about a foot long, diverge from a central point and are armed with brownish, radiating spines.

The Mohave cereus or cushion cactus (*C. mojavensis*) has long-spined stems about the size of baseballs, and these multiply until they form large cushions consisting of hundreds of stems; as many as 600 stems have been counted in a cluster. The flowers are a brilliant deep red. It is a species occupying rocky situations.

Of the echinocacti the huge barrel cactus (*Echinocactus acanthodes*) is most spectacular and best known. The great, stout stems, sometimes five or six but more often two or three feet high, are armed with strong, rigid spines which vary in color from bright red to yellow. This species reaches its best development on the gravelly fans of alluvium of the Colorado Desert. It grows in sheltered situations in the mountains of the Mohave Desert up to altitudes of 3,500 feet. Trade rats often completely hollow out the stems in their search for green food and water and leave only a "basket" of needles.

Closely allied to this is the Mohavean cotton-top or niggerhead (*E. polycephalus*), which forms compact, rounded clumps of elongate, ovoid heads, each eight or ten inches in diameter. The general color of the heads as seen from a short distance is purplish. The flowers, arranged in a crowning circle, are yellow, and the dry fruits are very woolly with white matted hairs. It prefers to grow among rocks.

Much less frequently seen are the two other species, *E. polyancistrus* and *E. johnsonii*. Both are plants of the upper Mohave Desert and the dry mountains northward. They have simple stems and the spines are without rings. The elongate stems (8 to 12 inches high) of *E. polyancistrus* are covered with many straight and also many hooked spines, the latter brownish. Johnson's cactus, sometimes called beehive cactus, has short, cylindrical stems, four to nine inches high, bearing many awl-shaped spines which are enlarged at the base.

The mammillaria or nipple cacti are so named because of the many teatlike tubercles on which the spines are borne. Of the five species known to the state of California, four occur on the deserts. They are divided into two groups—those with central spines hooked, and those with all the spines straight. Of those with hooked spines, *Mammillaria tetrancistra* is probably best known. It occurs on both deserts. Graham's fishhook cactus (*M. microcarpa*), having a white flower with a purple midvein, is confined wholly to the southern Colorado Desert. The straight-spined nipple cactus, *M. deserti*, grows in the mountains of the eastern Mohave Desert. The young plants are generally found half concealed in the gravel, but the neat attire of white, brown-tipped, interlocking spines makes them easy to find. The flowers, straw-colored or light lilac, open in late June. Alverson's mammillaria (*M. alversoni*), with light-purple flowers and with a dozen or more central, purple- or black-tipped spines to each nipple, is confined to the mountains to the north and east of the Salton Sea.

14. Trees

Where the conditions of aridity are intense, such as over the greater portion of the Mohave Desert and on rocky mesas and hillsides of the Colorado Desert, trees are usually absent, but where the ground-water supply is fairly abundant or plentiful, as in the large washes, along water courses, and about the margins of the Salton Sea, trees of low, spreading form flourish and often attain considerable dimensions. By observing these trees for size and luxuriance, it is possible to estimate with considerable accuracy the abundance and depth of underground waters.

One of the best of ground-water indicators is the honey, or straight-podded, mesquite (*Prosopis juliflora*), a desert tree of high water requirements found typically in aggregations in the alluvial soils of flood plains and lake basins and on sand dune edges. You will find a few of the trees about almost every fresh-water spring, no matter how isolated. Where the mesquite occurs in the dry beds of watercourses, it has served as one of the surest means of successfully locating places to dig wells. One of the worst insect enemies of this tree is the mesquite girdler (*Oncideres pustulatus*), a small, gray, long-haired beetle, with rust-colored spots on its back. The larvae burrow beneath the bark and the adults girdle the small stems. In either case the woody parts are eventually killed. The larvae of the round-headed mesquite borer (*Megacyllene antennatus*) work in the dry wood. These are white, robust grubs fully 1½ inches long, which quickly reduce the soundest cordwood to powder. Human woodcutters, in order to protect their wood, burn the bark and destroy the eggs. Many other insects live in or are associated with mesquite. Dr. E. O. Essig lists at least 25. Dr. P. H. Timberlake has collected in the Palm Springs area alone 12 species of small bees which visit the flowers of mesquite.

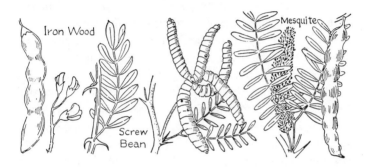

Closely allied to the honey, or straight-podded, mesquite, is the screw-bean (*Prosopis pubescens*), a small-stemmed tree first collected by Dr. Thomas Coulter on the old San Felipe Trail. It grows abundantly along the Colorado River, also along the watercourse of the Mohave River between Oro Grande and Daggett and again in Cave Canyon. Here the soil is deep and water is plentiful. In the Salton Sink it is common in almost pure stands near the north end of the Salton Sea. We encounter a few trees in sheltered canyon bottoms as far north as Death Valley. Trees in favored localities are known to grow to a height of 25 feet. The small holes often found in the curiously twisted seed pods of the screw-bean probably mark the exits of a small desert weevil (*Bruchus desertorum*) which breeds in the seeds of this and the honey mesquite. An Indian told me that these insect-infested pods were never discarded when the beans were ground up by the squaws to make the amole, or porridge.

The cat's-claw (*Acacia greggii*), most appropriately called "tear-blanket" and "wait-a-minute" by some of the other early travelers, is our only native acacia; like the acacias of the African deserts, it drops its leaves in the winter season (the Australian desert acacias are evergreen). In the wind-swept San Gorgonio Pass near Banning it occurs as a low, dense, spreading shrub scarcely more than 15 inches high; it shows most markedly the effects of exposure in modifying the form of plants. In the shelter of cliffs and in deep rock crevices it is a several-stemmed shrub, its slender, wandlike branches reaching a length of 6 or 7 feet. Its general habit is, however, more upright and it may become a tree fully 15 feet high. Its spiny branches afford a refuge for numerous small birds, the verdin being particularly partial to it when building its flask-shaped nest. The cat's-claw occurs in rocky washes and in gullies of the desert hillsides up to an altitude of 4,500 feet. The Providence Mountains mark its northern limit of occurrence. The wood is very hard and remarkably beautiful when finished.

Parasitic on both the mesquite and the cat's-claw as well as on the desert ironwood is a pendulous, slender-branched mistletoe (*Phoradendron californicum*). It bears plentiful supplies of white or waxy-red berries. This is the mistletoe responsible for the ill-health and final death of so many of the ironwood trees.

.Other tree members of the pea family are the three green-barked palo verdes (*Cercidium floridum, C. microphyllum,* and *Parkinsonia aculeata*). They occur as small shrubs to large trees in the detrital soil of the Colorado Desert washes and river bottoms, the *C. floridum* being generally distributed but *C. microphyllum* and *Parkinsonia aculeata* confined to the vicinity of the Colorado River. The leaves appear in

March but may occur on the trees at other times such as in late summer after deep-penetrating rains. The spring leaves may soon drop, leaving the showy, pale-yellow flowers and the smooth, vividly green bark as the trees' only adornment. In deep, sandy washes of the Chuckawalla district I have seen trees with crowns 40 feet across. The palo verde is very intolerant of frost, and this accounts for its absence from most of the Mohave Desert.

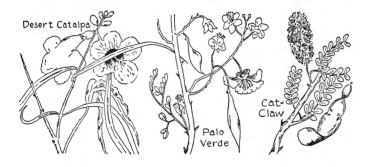

The legumes are further represented by the spiny, much-branched, broad-crowned desert ironwood (*Olneya tesota*), which flourishes in most of the large sand-washes and on the stream-dissected alluvial fans of the Colorado Desert from Indio southward into Sonora and Lower California and eastward into Arizona. In its form, it is extremely variable; particularly is this true of the older trees whose sturdy, blackish trunks seem bent at every conceivable angle. Owing to the injuries caused by mistletoe, the trunks and branches frequently show great, rounded swellings a foot or more in diameter. The fragrant lavender or purple flowers appear in May and June, and by August the flat seed pods are fat with the little brown seeds which in former years were so much prized by the Indians. Roasted, the seeds are said to have a rich, peanutlike flavor. When the young leaves first appear they are greatly relished by browsing animals, and in those happy days when we traveled about with donkeys we often tied the animals at night to a low, spreading tree, knowing for a certainty that their appetites would be well appeased by morning.

Although the dead ironwood is remarkably hard, the jaws of boring beetle larvae often reduce it to powder in a few months. The larvae of some beetles prefer, however, to work in the smaller branches. The wood of the dead trees makes the finest and most lasting of all campfires and often when away from the desert I long for the delicious odor of the smoke which is connected with so many pleasant memories of engaging experiences of bygone nights.

The smoke tree (*Parosela spinosa*), like the palo verde, enjoys strong summer suns and is intolerant of heavy frosts. Its northern limit of growth is found about ten miles north of the Union Pacific Railroad near Baker, California, and at the lower end of Death Valley. The seeds germinate very readily after summer rains and the sandy washes are populated with numerous tiny seedling trees which all too often die because of the ephemeral supplies of moisture. When moisture is permanent the trees grow to a height of 10 or 15 feet. In their dress of silver-green thorns and abundant fragrant ornamental bloom they are one of the show sights of the desert. The flowering season is usually mid-June. In the spring its spiny, leafless branches afford nesting sites for verdins, gnatcatchers, and thrashers. A moonlight night spent in a smoke-tree forest is an experience never to be forgotten.

In the late spring and summer days the desert catalpa or so-called desert willow (*Chilopsis linearis*) cheers the wayfarer with its pendant green leaves and its wealth of gay, pink, tubular flowers. It is largely confined to the edges and beds of washes where in the deep, well-drained sands some moisture lingers to dampen the long and often deep roots. The desert willow is the food plant of that remarkable moth, *Eucaterva variaria*, whose white wings on the upper side appear as if sprinkled with fine flakes of mica (see illustration, page 58). The larvae build tough, gauzy, buff-colored cases in which they pupate. The old cocoons, each about an inch long, are found still clinging to the small stems in spring like tiny Japanese paper lanterns.

Because of its great rarity in the California deserts the little-leaf elephant tree or torote (*Bursera microphylla*) when found is much acclaimed by visitors to the Anza-Borrego State Park. This woody tree of low stature, quite common in southwestern Arizona and in Lower California, has bright green aromatic foliage, tan-colored, peeling, parchmentlike bark, and massive trunk and branches.

The athel or flowering tamarisk (*Tamarix gallica*) has escaped from its original plantings on ranches and now occurs about many of the alkaline springs of Death Valley and irrigation canals of the Salton Basin. In places it may become an actual plant nuisance. The minute seeds, terminated by plumes of hairs, are probably distributed by both winds and birds.

Tamarix aphylla, the athel or salt cedar, often a large tree, is common about homes and roadsides of the Coachella and Imperial valleys where it is planted as a windbreak and for shade. The Southern Pacific Company has planted it extensively along its right-of-way between Whitewater and Indio to keep sand from blowing on the tracks. It is propagated by cuttings. Both kinds of tamarisk were brought in from the Mediterranean region.

In mountains high enough to support a growth of piñons, the desert scrub oak (*Quercus dumosa* var. *turbinella*) with its tiny gray leaves is found. In some of the high valleys of the Little San Bernardino Mountains it forms a tree of generous proportions.

Rarest of all our arid-mountain trees is the hackberry (*Celtis douglasii*), known on the deserts of California only from a few localities in far eastern San Bernardino County. I have found it on Clark Mountain and in the New York Mountains.

One occasionally meets a few specimens of the Arizona ash (*Fraxinus velutina*) or its leather-leaved variety, *coriacea*, along the desert streams and about springs. It is a Great Basin tree common in southern Utah and southern Nevada. The dwarf ash (*F. anomala*) is a species so un-ashlike that it is always a puzzler to the novice in tree lore. The leaves, instead of being compound, are usually simple and roundish, from one and a half to two inches across. It is truly a desert species and may be found, as a shrub or small tree, along washes of Clark Mountain and in the Providence and the Panamint ranges.

The Washingtonia palm (*Washingtonia filifera*) is a native tree of the Salton Basin and its bordering mountains. The extensive groves found north of Indio along the line of the San Andreas fault have been repeatedly burned by vandals until their former beauty is gone. Many small groups, still untouched and fortunately undiscovered by the public, lie hidden about water seeps in many of the little canyons in the Santa Rosa Range. The palm is an unfailing sign of the presence of water, but the quality is not necessarily good, since the trees are very tolerant of alkali. The first printed record of the finding of the Washingtonia palm is in *Emory's Reconnaissance* (1848). The party of weary travelers crossing the Colorado Desert had passed its western portals and after having journeyed a few miles beyond a spring called Ojo Grande, they met palms. "Here," says Emory, "on November 29, several scattered objects were seen projected against the cliffs and hailed by the Florida campaigners, some of whom were along, as old friends. They were the cabbage trees and marked the locale of a spring and a small patch of grass." This place at the head of Carrizo Creek Canyon is now known as Palm Springs. Then, as now, the moist plot about the palms was probably sodded with salt grass (*Distichlis spicata*), wire rush (*Juncus balticus*), and a sedge (*Scirpus americana*) known as "three-square" because of its triangular stems.

Dried and drying palms are quite often found to be infested by the larvae of a robust bostrychid beetle (*Dinapate wrightii*), the California palm borer. The large galleries where the larvae fed and later pupated are regular features of old, weathered palm logs. The finger-sized holes in the logs are places where the adult beetles emerged.

In the rocky hills bordering the Colorado River, from the Riverside Mountains southward toward Yuma, and at the far eastern end of the Little Chuckawalla Mountains a few specimens of the giant sahuaros (*Cereus gigantea*) grow. They are California's largest cacti, and it is hoped the few specimens will long be preserved. The distribution of this cactus is delimited westward by the lack of summer rains such as occur in Arizona, Sonora, and Lower California. The little elf owl, so common in southern Arizona, finding suitable environment here, lives in many of the deserted woodpecker holes found in the robust stems.

The tree yucca or Joshua tree (*Yucca brevifolia*) and its subspecies *Jaegeriana* is at once the most spectacular and most characteristic tree of the Mohave Desert. In its various forms it occurs north through the high mountainous areas of the Death Valley region and eastward into Nevada, Utah, and Arizona; its southeasternmost station in California is, I believe, in the Iron Mountains of eastern Riverside County, where a few trees grow along the Aqueduct road between Boulder Well and Rice. It reaches its point of most southern distribution in the Joshua Tree National Monument. As was the case with the Washingtonia palm, this yucca was given the name of cabbage tree by the pioneer travelers, and today it is often erroneously brigaded with the palms under the name of "yucca palm." The biology of this bizarre tree is still very imperfectly known and I have spent some very interesting hours studying the root system, noting the rapidity of its growth, and collecting the insects which congregate about the fruits and flowers, or bore, as larvae, in its sturdy branches. The two chief causes of branching of the tree yucca appear to be the dying of the terminal buds after flowering and the injury caused by the yucca-boring weevil (*Scyphophorus yuccae*). The larvae of this beetle, when ready for pupation, build in the ends of the branches peculiar, tough cases of frass, as the chewed-up, fibrous refuse from boring insects is called. The so-called petrified wood, much prized as fuel by desert settlers, is made by the plant as it lays down silica in the cell walls in its attempt to wall off the injuries done by the borers, by fire, or by wind.

This tree propagates itself by means of seed and by sending out long, underground runners. We are especially interested in the young plants that spring from the runners, for it is upon these that the Navaho yucca borer (a butterfly, *Megathymus yuccae navaho*) lays her large eggs. When these hatch, the energetic larvae bore into the young plants and make their way to the larger underground stems, where they feed and later pupate. The female butterfly seems to know that if she lays her eggs on the small-rooted, small-stemmed plants which spring from seeds there will be no food there for her larvae. In some uncanny way she is able to distinguish between the seedling plants and the runner plants—a distinction which man cannot readily make! Because the plants of runner origin alone are suited to her needs, the female, so far as is known, never lays her eggs upon the seedling plants.

The scrub juniper (*J. californica*) of the western Mohave and Colorado deserts, the Utah juniper (*J. osteosperma*) mostly of the eastern desert ranges, and the single-leaf piñon (*Pinus monophylla*) are among the most drought-resistant of our cone-bearing trees. They occur on most of the higher desert ranges that reach an elevation of 5,000 feet or over, often forming a fairly dense cover, particularly in deep, granitic soils. In the New York Mountains of eastern San Bernardino

County, they associate with the two-needle nut-pine (*P. edulis*). Since the nuts of piñon trees are eagerly sought as food by rodents, human nut-hunters must be early in the field to get their share. The usual pine-nut harvest season is the middle of September. The commonest mistletoe of the scrub junipers is *Phoradendron bolleanum* var. *densum*, the compact clumps of which adorn almost every tree. In the Piñon-Juniper Woodland along the western edge of the Colorado Desert and into Lower California grows the Parry Piñon (*P. quadrifolia = P. Parryana*) with leaves mostly in bundles of fours, a tree unusually trim and shapely when young.

The water-loving willows and cottonwoods thrust their roots into the moist soils of streamways and mark the location of a great number of the isolated springs found in canyon bottoms or on rocky hillsides. The cottonwoods (*Populus fremonti*) along the Mohave River intermittently mark the stream's long course through the desert as far east as Cave Canyon. In the branches of this cheerful tree hang long festoons of a mistletoe with yellowish-green leaves (*Phoradendron flavescens* var. *macrophyllum*). A peculiar, long-leaved variety of this cottonwood (*P. fremonti* var. *arizonica*) is found on the desert's edge at Snow Creek in the San Jacinto Mountains. The tall, handsome, slender-branched cottonwood of the Colorado delta, now so commonly planted along city streets and about ranches in the Imperial and Coachella valleys, is the MacDougall cottonwood (*P. fremonti* var. *MacDougallii*). It was introduced into the Salton Sink by the Southern Pacific Company. Trees brought from Yuma were planted about the stations.

Forestiera (*F. neo-mexicana*) is a small tree belonging to the same great natural group as the olive. The bark is smooth, the leaves are simple, and the branches are opposite. This tree has a tendency to be gregarious, and small groups of them occur here and there in the high desert canyons.

15. Travel Hints

It has become a habit among writers to describe the desert as a region of desolation, cheerless and dreary, a land of relentless heat, with every plant vested in thorns and every animal poisonous or savage. They have dwelt upon the difficulties and perils of travel in mule-and-wagon days and would have us think that it is equally difficult today to make our way by auto over the miles of desert roads. As a matter of fact, the desert is on the whole a friendly land, its beasts no fiercer than those found elsewhere; nor is travel in it, except in rare instances, unusually dangerous for those who use discretion in taking care of themselves and their motor cars. Several of the main highways are paved, and many of the minor "roads which lead to nowhere" are easily negotiated by the circumspect traveler.

Hazlitt reminds us that "there is nothing so pleasing as going on a journey." This is particularly true when the journey takes one to the unspoiled, untilled desert. There one is free of all ties, and if he is fortunate enough to have in any measure the spirit of the artist, the naturalist, or the mystic, his days of travel will be filled with wonder. The desert landscape is monotonous only to the uninformed.

Autumn and winter days are best for visits to the low-lying

Colorado Desert. The winter nights may be nippy with cold, but the balmy, sunny days make one wish he might live perpetually in this out-of-door land of paradise. March marks the onset of the flower season, and then the whole country may be aglow with color and the air heavy with the sweet perfume of sand verbenas, evening primroses, and encelias. When in the warmth of April days the annuals of the Salton Basin begin to wilt and turn brown, the Mohavean blossoms are at their best. They continue blooming until late in May.

Halcyon days cannot be expected to last forever. All too frequently the times of quiet weather are interrupted by days of wind. The desert traveler must either learn to enjoy from time to time the wind's weird music and wild ways or leave the desert when the blustery days of the flower season arrive.

Even summer offers attractions to those who appreciate calm evenings, cloudless night skies, and fine, clear mornings. I prefer to avoid the heat of midday, but often in July and August I slip over the mountain passes to spend the night on the desert's edge. If the motor car is equipped for sleeping, or if one has a high cot, he need not fear that snakes or other creeping things will share the blankets with him. I must draw attention, though, to the danger of walking abroad on warm nights without a lantern or a flashlight, for it is certain that snakes are active then.

Really to appreciate the desert you must live close to its heart, walk upon its unbroken soil, and camp upon its clean sands. In choosing a campsite, the first thought should be given to finding shelter from possible wind and a level, open place for the fire and the bed. I usually take to the sandy washes, where large smoke trees, palo verdes, and mesquites furnish wood and noonday shade. I often find delightful sheltered spots in the lee of great rocks or along the walls of canyons. In winter days the pockets along the edge of lava flows offer covert. Having five gallons of water with me, I am free to camp wherever I please.

Illustrative of day or week-end trips on which little more than a sight-seeing program is undertaken is the tour from Los Angeles to Indio on the Colorado Desert, or to Red Rock Canyon, or to Barstow, Mitchell's Caverns, and the Kelso Sand Dunes on the Mohave Desert. If several days are at one's disposal, real holiday journeys to Death Valley (4 days), to Lone Pine and Darwin (3 days), to El Centro and Yuma (3 days), or to Needles (3 days) are in order. The journey to Death Valley* is particularly delightful since it furnishes such a rich variety of scenic beauty. From November until May the trip may be made in comfort. To see the country to best advantage one should go by way of Barstow, Baker, and Silver Lake and return through Lone Pine or Trona. If one desires a dash of human interest, he can visit some of the old mining camps, settle down for a few days at a place such as Ballarat or Darwin, and get acquainted with some of the good-natured inhabitants of those out-of-the-way corners of the desert domain.

From Indio the vacationist can reach the Borrego Desert and the Salton Sea, the beautiful sandstone and clay hills to the east of Mecca, the rolling dunes near Yuma; and, nearer

* Death Valley was constituted a National Monument by Presidential proclamation in February 1933. It comprises an area of 3,103 square miles, or 2,000,000 acres, and has as its peculiar interests a unique flora and marvelously interesting and beautiful geological formations. According to Dr. L. F. Noble, it contains "rocks of all the great geological time divisions—Archean, Paleozoic, Mesozoic, Tertiary and Quaternary—whose aggregate thickness certainly exceeds 30,000 feet for the stratified rocks alone. Earth movements in the area have been so profound and so recurrent that the rock masses form a complex mosaic of crustal blocks isolated one from another by folding, faulting, tilting, igneous intrusion, erosion and buried under Quaternary alluvium." It is truly a geologist's paradise. The serious student will do well to read Dr. Noble's paper, 'Rock Formations of Death Valley, California," *Science*, August 24, 1934. The author's book, *A Naturalist's Death Valley*, Publication # 5, Death Valley 49's, Inland Printing and Engraving, San Bernardino 1964, will provide information of a general nature.

at hand, the scenic, palm-inhabited canyons of Mount San Jacinto.

On the Los Angeles–Lone Pine tour one sees to advantage the magnificent erosional forms of Red Rock Canyon, spacious dry lakes, tinted volcanic craters and black lava flows, and, at last, Owens Lake, the escarpment of the Inyo Range, and the steep granite wall of the majestic Sierra Nevada.

The journey to Needles acquaints one with the broad depressions of the mid-Mohave region, its strange, picturesque, fan-encircled mountain forms, black cinder cones, recent lava flows, and the broad flood plains of the Colorado River.

The principal points of interest on the Las Vegas road are the vari-tinted Calico Mountains, the Lake Manix clay beds, the magnificent Cima Dome, Soda Lake, and, as the California border is reached, the strange mountains of banded limestones.

A large area of about one million acres, for the most part in Riverside County, was early in 1937 set aside as the Joshua Tree National Monument. It embraces a wide variety of biological environments ranging from near sea level to 5,000-feet altitude. Its plants and animals are of both Great Basin and Sonoran affinities and represent many species not found in the more northern Death Valley Monument. The area is one of splendid scenic beauty, with remarkable rock formations, deep canyons, and broad desert basins. From Inspiration Point, sometimes called Keys' View, one gains a comprehensive view of the marvelous Salton Basin such as can be gained from few other eminences. A week or an entire month spent here in spring or autumn will yield rich rewards to the intelligent traveler.

Since one knows intimately only the country he has walked over, take my hint: abandon the motor car as soon as possible and travel on foot. Then you will move in a leisurely manner, confine your wanderings to a small area, and enter into profitable intimacy with nature. Go alone on your walks if you can, but if you must take a companion, choose one who will appreciate with you the desert's great silence.

Early in the day when the senses are keen and fresh, take to climbing the mountains. The higher you climb, the more marvelous is the prospect. The country now acquires new importance, and every mountain range seen in the distance invites exploration.

16. The Preservation of Deserts

Our beautiful deserts are wholly the creation of nature. Some of them are among the most appealing of our scenic wonderlands. Their broad basins and long intermountain valleys, their bizarre land forms such as volcanic buttes, mesas, bajadas, and often barren but majestic mountains, rising like colorful spires from the low sweep of creosote bush and sagebrush, are places which, left undisturbed, minister greatly to the pleasure and ennoblement of man's mind.

Here are lands of expansive vistas, of exceedingly clear, clean skies, sometimes flecked with clouds brilliantly white. Here we see mountains charmingly colored in pastel shades of blue or magenta, and after ample summer or winter rains, look upon huge expanses of floral color.

Most unfortunate it is that, perhaps more than any portion of our land heritage, our deserts are thought of by many as the most expendable lands we possess, mere wastelands that should if possible be utilized for gain. Even to many "conservationists," conservation means only efficient exploitation of the land, getting everything possible out of it while perpetuating enough of what is left to serve as "seed" for suc-

This chapter is adapted from an article by the author in *The Nature Conservancy News*, Vol. XIV (1964), No. 3.

cessive exploitations. To these persons the terms "yield" and "harvest" are much-used and sacred words. They look upon nature with satisfaction only so long as it can yield financial returns, feed more animals and human beings, provide clothing and shelter, and supply means for paid recreation for man. They would almost completely make over nature, leaving the "man-did-it-look" upon almost every part of it. They regard almost every part of the yet-untouched desert as near to worthless, but if possible, they say, it must be supplied with water for growing crops or provided with "improvements" where people can live and engage in pay-recreation of the man-made sort such as golfing, hunting, and fishing. They appreciate very little nature's true amenities.

Up to now the once-beautiful deserts of southern California, southern Arizona, and southern Nevada with their warm winter climates have been utilized most for agriculture and for building and subdivision. I fear that the tendency to "develop" there is irreversible: there is too much money to be made by it. As irrigation waters are further made available by desalinization of sea water and the building of vast systems of aqueducts and upland reservoirs, very few enclaves of primitive beauty can be saved. Owing to the destruction of natural habitats, many native birds, insects, and mammals must forever disappear.

Another great menace to desert preservation is the activities of the military establishments, which have had truly vast areas in the far western states reserved for their activities and are continually seeking the reservation of new desert lands. Instead of cooperating and combining their efforts and together utilizing the enormous areas already set aside for them, each branch of the services desires its own huge land area.

The year 1964 witnessed the very grave destruction of the middle and eastern Mohave Desert in an activity called Desert Strike, in which a hundred thousand men and numerous kinds of heavy equipment milled around for nearly a month, often utterly destroying desert vegetation, wildlife, and wildlife habitats over an enormous area. It appears that little if any thought was given to the preservation of the natural amenities of this magnificent sweep of fragile desert. Not in a hundred years can the damage be repaired by nature even if no further such exercises take place.

Poorly conceived, still more poorly administered, was the desert small-tract act sometimes called the Jack-rabbit Homestead Act. Instead of giving week-end desert homes to people who love and respect the desert, it became the opportunity for speculators, who for a fee located tract sites and then sold to people (often speculators themselves) miserably planned and flimsily built boxlike structures, which were erected by the tens of thousands, dotting the landscape like mushrooms and making a horrible festering eyesore. Most of the tract homes were never occupied even for a night and very soon became subject to vandalism. Now the paint is peeling, roofs have been blown off by the strong winds, windows and doors are gone, and some of the small shacks have been burned.

Some county planning commissions have designated large areas of remote desert lands for future use by heavy industry, feeling that noxious gases and air-polluting dust would do little harm, or the dumping of wastes would not arouse public anger.

Los Angeles City at one time sought the right to run long daily trains carrying garbage, street litter, and other city wastes to the Colorado Desert, there to dump it. Fortunately the municipality was defeated in its efforts. But the indiscriminate casting off of garbage and litter by individuals living on the desert still goes on: it is a very widespread practice. Sometimes folks drive many miles to find some rock formation or wash, often very beautiful ones, in which to dispose of their waste, and there it stays for many years. In the dry air, tin cans are slow to rust, the old mattresses, chairs, and whatnots last on and on; broken pottery and glass last indefinitely. In damp climates some of the trash might disintegrate or at least be covered by kindly disposed vegetation which would spring up and, as if ashamed of man, try to cover it.

The late winter and spring herding of sheep, brought in in great numbers from as far away as Idaho, Nevada, and Montana by means of railroads and trucks, has presented a great conservation and preservation problem. The "four-footed locusts" are particularly destructive to the annual wildflower fields, since they leave little but hoof-trampled dusty ground behind them and eat almost all the ripening seeds. Not only public lands but private properties suffer from this grazing of sheep. Property owners protesting mightily have recently been given some protection in San Bernardino County by an ordinance which makes the sheepowners responsible for damages if they allow their animals to graze on private lands without a permit from the landowner. It has made sheepherders much more careful about where they operate.

The Desert Protective Council with its more than 800 members has done valiant service in protecting the amenities of our deserts. Initially it was organized to oppose the efforts of persistent commercial interests to build a short-cut road through the heart of the Joshua Tree National Monument and thus channel trade from the U.S. Marine base near Twentynine Palms to the Coachella Valley. In this opposition the council was successful, and since then it has from year to year marked up many other accomplishments in protecting our deserts from exploiters and in encouraging desert preservation. This well-respected and influential organization of devoted desert lovers has sponsored lectures, circulated educational leaflets, worked hand in hand with other conservation organizations, thwarted efforts to despoil the desert of its wildflower fields, originated and encouraged the passage and enforcement of laws protecting desert animals (particularly the desert tortoise) and trees. It has also been a leader in getting portions of desert lands set aside for parks and wholesome recreational activities.

In proposing desert nature reserves, we should think of small ones as well as large ones. Small reserves of several to a hundred acres to protect a particular landmark or other natural feature can be very satisfying. But large ones are most to be sought, for desert connotes vastness, great sweeps of land untouched by the often grimy hand of man, who is given to taking over the land and cluttering it with his "developments" of roads, subdivisions, etc.

Even large reserves such as Joshua Tree National Monument, Anza-Borrego State Park, and Death Valley need to be increased in size *now,* before it is forever too late. There must be more and more places where people driving two-wheeled vehicles and jeeps cannot tear up the land by racing unrestricted over desert stretches for the mere satisfaction of raising dust, moving swiftly, or jolting the body. These people usually take more delight in frightening wild game than in observing the ways of shy wilderness denizens.

All too often public agencies planning desert parks think mostly in terms of picnic tables, impractical stone stoves, shelters from sun, and restrooms—the same kinds of conveniences provided in parks, in the forests, at seashores, and in areas close to cities. These may be good in their place, but they are hardly what nature admirers and preservers of the charm of desert wilderness like to see encouraged on any large scale.

An ideal desert preserve, especially if it is a small one, should provide only the minimum of camping facilities. It is enough to have a very few access roads which reach only to the perimeters. Water need not be provided. Let people bring their water even as they bring their food. In order are a few nature trails to educate people concerning the natural history of deserts and a center where lectures can be given by competent leaders.

Selected References

Atwood, Wallace A. *The Physiographic Provinces of North America*. Boston: Ginn and Company, 1940.

Austin, Mary. *Land of Little Rain*. Boston: Houghton Mifflin, 1903.

Bailey, Vernon. "Harmful and Beneficial Mammals of the Arid Interior," *United States Department of Agriculture Farmers Bulletin No. 335*, 1908.

————. "Sources of Water Supply for Desert Animals," *Scientific Monthly*, XVII (1923), 66–86.

Bassett, Allen M., and Kupfer, Donald H. *A Geologic Reconnaissance in the Southeastern Mohave Desert*. Special Report, California Division of Mines and Geology. Ferry Building, San Francisco, 1964.

Bates, Marston. *Animal Worlds*. New York; Random House, 1963.

Benson, Lyman, and Darrow, Robert. *A Manual of Southwestern Trees and Shrubs*. Tucson: University of Arizona, 1944.

Biology of Deserts. London Institute of Biology, 1954.

Brown, J. S. "Routes to Desert Watering Places in the Salton Sea Region, California," *United States Geological Survey Water-Supply Paper 490-A*, 1920.

Burt, William H., and Grossenheider, Richard P. *A Field Guide to the Mammals*. Boston: Houghton Mifflin, 1952.

Buxton, P. A. *Animal Life in Deserts*. London: E. Arnold & Co., 1923.

Cahalane, Victor H. *Mammals of North America*. New York: Macmillan, 1947.

Camp, C. L. "Notes on the Local Distribution and Habits of the Amphibians and Reptiles of Southeastern California in the Vicinity of the Turtle Mountains," *University of California Publications in Zoölogy*, XII (1916), 503–43.

Campbell, Elizabeth W. Crozer. "An Archeological Survey of the Twentynine Palms Region," *Southwest Museum Papers, No. 7*, 1931.

————. "Pinto Basin Site, An Ancient Aboriginal Camping Ground in the California Desert," *Southwest Museum Papers, No. 9*, 1935.

Cannon, W. A. *Root Habits of Desert Plants*. Washington, D.C.: Carnegie Institution of Washington, 1911.

Carter, Francis. "Bird Life at Twentynine Palms," *Condor,* Vol. XXXIX (1937), No. 5.

Chase, J. S. *California Desert Trails.* Boston: Houghton Mifflin, 1919.

Chew, R. M. "Water Metabolism of Desert Inhabiting Vertebrates," *Biological Reviews,* XXXVI (1961), 1–31.

Cloudsley-Thompson, J. L., and Chadwick, M. J. *Life in Deserts.* Dufour Editions, Chester Springs, Pa., 1964.

Coues, Elliot. *Birds of the Colorado Valley.* Washington, D.C.: Government Printing Office, 1878.

Coville, F. V. "Botany of the Death Valley Expedition," *Contributions from the United States National Herbarium, No. 4,* 1893.

Cowles, Raymond B. "Notes on the Ecology and Breeding Habits of the Desert Minnow, *Cyprinodon macularius," Copeia,* No. 1, 1934.

Darton, N. H., and others. "Guidebook of the Western United States, Part C, Santa Fe Route," *United States Geological Survey Bulletin 613,* 1916.

Davis, Wm. Morris. "Basin Range Types," *Science,* LXXVI (1932), 241–45.

————. "Granitic Domes of the Mohave Desert, California," *Transactions of the San Diego Society of Natural History,* Vol. VII (1933), No. 20, pp. 211–58.

Desert Research. Research Council of Israel, Special Publication No. 2. Jerusalem: Research Council of Israel, 1953.

Dodge, Natt N. *Flowers of the Southwest Deserts.* Santa Fe: Southwestern Monuments Association, 1947.

Gale, H. S. "Salines in the Owens, Searles, and Panamint Basins, Southeastern California," *United States Geological Survey Bulletin 580,* 1915, pp. 251–323.

Geology of Southern California. Bulletin 170, Vols. I and II. California Division of Mines and Geology, Ferry Building, San Francisco, 1954.

Grinnell, Joseph. "An Account of the Mammals and Birds of the Lower Colorado Valley," *University of California Publications in Zoölogy,* Vol. XV (1915).

————. "Further Observations upon the Bird Life of Death Valley," *Condor,* Vol. XXXVI, March 1934.

Harder, E. C. "Iron-Ore Deposits of the Eagle Mountains, California," *United States Geological Survey Bulletin 503,* 1912.

Herre, A. W. C. T. "Lichens, Impossible Plants," *Scientific Monthly,* Vol. XVI (1923), No. 2, pp. 130–40.

Hoffman, Ralph. *Birds of the Pacific States.* Boston: Houghton Mifflin, 1927.

Hornaday, W. T. *Campfires on Desert and Lava.* New York: Scribner's, 1908.

Huntington, Ellsworth. *Civilization and Climate.* New Haven: Yale University Press, 1924.

Jaeger, Edmund C. *Desert Wild Fowers.* Rev. ed. Stanford: Stanford University Press, 1964.

————. *Our Desert Neighbors.* Stanford: Stanford University Press, 1950.

————. *The North American Deserts.* Stanford: Stanford University Press, 1957.

————. *Desert Wildlife.* Stanford: Stanford University Press, 1961.

————. *A Naturalist's Death Valley.* Pub. No. 5, Death Valley 49's. San Bernardino: Inland Printers and Engravers, 1964.

Johnson, David, Bryant, Monroe D., and Miller, Alden H. *Vertebrate Animals of the Providence Mountains Area of California.* Berkeley: University of California Press, 1948.

Kirk, Ruth. *Exploring Death Valley.* 2d ed. Stanford: Stanford University Press, 1965.

Klauber, L. M. "A Key to the Rattlesnakes with Summary of Characteristics," *Transactions of the San Diego Society of Natural History,* Vol. VIII (1936), No. 20.

Kroeber, A. L. *Handbook of the Indians of California.* Washington, D.C.: Government Printing Office, 1925.

Lawson, A. C. "The Epigene Profiles of the Desert," *University of California Department of Geology Bulletin,* IX (1915), 37–38.

Longwell, Chester, Knopf, Adolph, and Flint, Richard. *A Textbook of Geology.* New York: John Wiley & Sons, 1932.

Louderback, Geo. D. "Basin Range Structure in the Great Basin," *University of California Publications in Geology,* Vol. XIV (1923), No. 10.

Loudermilk, J. D. "On the Origin of Desert Varnish," *American Journal of Science,* XXI (1931), 51–65.

Macdougal, D. T. *Botanical Features of North American Deserts.* Washington, D.C.: Carnegie Institution of Washington, 1908.

Mallery, T. D. "Rainfall Records for the Sonoran Desert," *Ecology,* Vol. XVII (1936), Nos. 1 and 2.

Manly, W. L. *Death Valley in '49*. San Jose, Calif.: Pacific Tree and Vine Company, 1894.

Maxon, John H. *Death Valley, Origin and Scenery*. Bishop, Calif.: Chalfant Press, 1963.

McKelvey, Susan Delano. "Notes on Yucca," *Journal of the Arnold Arboretum*, Vol. XVI, 1935.

Meinzer, O. E. "Map of the Pleistocene Lakes of the Basin and Range Province and Its Significance," *Bulletin of the Geological Society of America*, XXXIII (1922), 541–52.

Mendenhall, W. C. "Groundwaters of the Indio Region, California, with a Sketch of the Colorado Desert," *United States Geological Survey Water-Supply Paper 225*, 1909.

————. "Some Desert Watering Places in Southeastern California and Southwestern Nevada," *United States Geological Survey Water-Supply Paper 224*, 1909.

Merriam, J. C. "Extinct Faunas of the Mohave Desert," *Popular Science*, LXXXVI (1915), 245–64.

Miller, Alden H., and Stebbins, Robert C. *The Lives of Desert Animals in Joshua Tree National Monument*. Berkeley: University of California Press, 1964.

Miller, Loye. "Notes on the Desert Tortoise," *Transactions of the San Diego Society of Natural History*, Vol. VII (1932), No. 18.

Mosauer, Walter. "The Reptiles of a Sand Dune Area and Its Surroundings in the Colorado Desert," *Ecology*, Vol. XVI (1935), No. 1.

Murie, Olaus. *A Field Guide to Animal Tracks*. Boston: Houghton Mifflin Company, 1954.

Noble, L. F. "Note on a Colemanite Deposit near Shoshone, California, with a Sketch of a Part of Amargosa Valley," *United States Geological Survey Bulletin 785*, 1926.

Norris, Kenneth S. "The Ecology of the Desert Iguana, *Dipsosaurus dorsalis*," *Ecology*, Vol. XXXIV (1953), No. 2.

Norris, Robert M., and Norris, Kenneth S. "Algodones Dunes of Southern California," *Geological Society of America Bulletin*, LXXII (1961), 605–60.

Palmer, T. S. *Chronology of the Death Valley Region in California, 1849–1949*. Privately printed, 1952.

Palmer, William R. *Pahute Indian Legends*. Salt Lake City: Deseret Book Company, 1946.

Parish, S. B. "Vegetation of the Mohave and Colorado Deserts of Southern California," *Ecology,* Vol. XI (1930), No. 3.

Parker, Ronald B. *Recent Vulcanism at Amboy Crater, San Bernardino County, California.* Special Report No. 76, California Division of Mines and Geology. Ferry Building, San Francisco, 1963.

Peterson, Roger Tory. *A Field Guide to Western Birds.* 2d. ed. Boston: Houghton Mifflin, 1961.

Rogers, Malcolm J. "Report of an Archaeological Reconnaissance in the Mohave Sink Region," *Archeology,* Vol. I (1929), No. 1.

————. "Yuman Pottery Making," *San Diego Museum Papers, No. 2,* 1936.

Saunders, Charles F. *The Southern Sierras of California.* Boston: Houghton Mifflin, 1923.

Shreve, Forrest. "The Plant Life of the Sonoran Desert," *Scientific Monthly,* March 1936.

————. "The Problems of the Desert," *Scientific Monthly,* March 1934.

————. *Vegetation of the Sonoran Desert.* Washington, D.C.: Carnegie Institution of Washington, 1951.

Shreve, Forrest, and Mallery, T. D. "The Relation of Caliche to Desert Plants," *Soil Science,* Vol. XXXV (1933), No. 2.

Spaulding, V. M. *Distribution and Movements of Desert Plants.* Washington, D.C.: Carnegie Institution of Washington, 1909.

Spurr, J. E. "Descriptive Geology of Nevada South of the Fortieth Parallel and Adjacent Portions of California," *United States Geological Survey Bulletin 208,* 1903.

Stebbins, Robert C. *Amphibians and Reptiles of Western North America.* New York: McGraw-Hill, 1954.

Sumner, F. B. "Some Biological Problems of Our Southwestern Deserts," *Ecology,* VI (1925), 352–71.

Thompson, David G. "The Mohave Desert Region, California," *United States Geological Survey Water-Supply Paper 578,* 1929.

Thorpe, W. H. "Miscellaneous Records of Insects Inhabiting the Saline Waters of the California Desert Regions," *Pan-Pacific Entomologist,* Vol. VII (1931), No. 4.

Tidestrom, I. "Flora of Utah and Nevada," *Contributions from the United States National Herbarium, No. 25,* 1925.

Van Dyke, J. C. *Desert: Further Studies in Natural Appearances.* New York: Scribner's, 1901.

Vorhies, C. T. "Poisonous Animals of the Desert," *Arizona University Agricultural Experiment Station Bulletin, No. 83,* 1917.

Walther, J. *Das Gesetz der Wüstenbildung.* 4th ed. Leipzig, 1924.

Waring, G. A. "Ground-Water in Pahrump and Ivanpah Valleys, Nevada and California," *United States Geological Survey Water-Supply Paper 450,* 1920.

Weber, John Milton. *Yuccas of the Southwest,* Agriculture Monographs No. 17, U.S.D.A., 1952.

Index

Index

Aborigines, 112–21
Amargosa Desert, 72
Amargosa River, 13
Amitermes, 45
Amphibians, 67
Ant lions, 46
Ants, 53–55
Arenivaga, 45
Aridity, intensity of, 41
Anza-Borrego State Park, 193
Ash, 179, 180
Atriplex, 164
Attinie, 55

Bailey, Vernon, 103, 109
Barchanes, 27
Bees, 52, 53
Beetles, 50–52
Beloperone, 163
Birds, 84–98
Blackbirds, 90
Blake, W. P., 120
Bonneville, Lake, 7
Bootettix, 41
Bufo, 68, 69
Buprestidae, 51
Burroweed, 158, 161
Butterflies, 55–57
Buxton, P. A., 2, 41, 43

Cacti, 167–74; barrel cactus, 172;
    Cereus, 171; *Mammillaria*, 173;
    nipple cactus, 173; *Opuntia*, 170,
    171
Calico Mountains, 31
Callisaurus, 73
Cat's-claw, 176
Cattails, 157
Cercidium, 176, 177
Chalcedon checkerspot, 56
Cheilanthes, 47

Cicada killer, 48
Cicadas, 48
Cima Dome, 23
Cinder cones, 20–22
Cnemidophorus, 74
Cockroaches, 45
Colorado Desert: defined 3, 14;
    weather, 34–41
Conservation of deserts, 189
Cottonwood, 183
Coyote, 107
Coyote wells, 26
Creosote bush, 159, 160; gall-
    midge, 160
Cricket, sand treader, 44
Crickets, 44, 45
Crotalus, 82
Crucifixion thorn, 166
Cuddleback Arch, 24
Culex, 49
Cyprinodon, 66

Dalea, 161, 178
Dasymutilla, 155
Death Valley, 39, 186
Desert Strike, 190, 191
Desert varnish, 153
Deserts: causes of, definition, geo-
    logic history, location of, 1–7;
    physiographic aspects, 17
Dinothrombidium, 61, 62
Dipsosaurus, 61
Dragonflies, 46
Dry lakes, 25
Dunes: Algodones, 26, 27; elephant,
    27; Kelso, 26, 30

Earth star (*Geaster*), 151
Earwig, 58
Elephant tree, 179
Emory, W. H., 165, 174, 189

Ephedra (desert tea), 160
Ephydrid flies, 49
Evaporation-rainfall ratio, 41

Falcon, prairie, 96
Fault-block mountains, 18
Faults, 18–20
Ferns, 153–55
Fishes, 66, 67
Flicker, red-shafted, 85
Flies, 48, 49
Flora: genera and species, 122–49;
   illustrations identifying, 127-49;
   origin of desert, 124, 125
Flower season, 122, 123
Flycatcher, vermillion, 90
Forestiera, 183
Fouquieria, 166, 167
Foxes, 107, 108
Franseria, 161
Frogs, 69
Fungi, 150, 151

Gall-fly, 160
Gall-midge, creosote, 160
Galls, 160
Gambusia, 66
Garcés, Father Francisco, 116, 121
Garlock Fault, 18
Geaster, 151
Gecko, banded, 77
Gnatcatcher, 85
Goat-nut, 161, 162
"Goblet valleys," 19
Goldfinches, 85
Goose, Canada, 86, 87
Gopher snake, 83
Gophers, 106
Granddaddy longlegs, 63, 64
Granite rocks, 23
Grasses, 156, 157; frost grass, 157;
   galleta grass, 156; needle grass,
   157; red bromus, 157; rice grass,
   156; salt grass, 157
Grasshoppers, 44

Ground squirrel: antelope, 105;
   round-tailed, 105
Gypsum, 29

Hackberry, 179, 180
Harvestmen, 63, 64
Hawks: marsh, 87; Western red-
   tailed, 96; sparrow, 97
Heat, 39
Helminthoglypta, 65
Hilaria, 156
Hippaletes, 48
Holly, desert, 164
Honey ants, 55
Hop sage, 160
Humidiy, 38, 39
Hummingbirds, 92
Hyla, 69
Hymenoclea, 162

Illustrations, see under Wild
   flowers of the desert
Indians, 112–21; Chemehuevi, 116;
   Koso, 117, 118; Mohave, 115, 116,
   119; Panamint, 116, 117; Serrano,
   120; Shoshone, 115; Vanyume,
   121; Yuma, 115, 118, 120
Insects, 42–58
Ironwood, 177, 178
Isomeris, 163

Jack rabbit, 106, 107
Joshua tree, 23, 181, 182
Juniper, 182

Kangaroo rats, 100, 101
Kelso dunes, 26
Kit fox, 107, 108
Krameria, 161

Lac-scale, 47
Lake areas of Great Basin, 6–13
Lake Lahontan, 7
Lake Bonneville, 7
Lake Le Conte, 14, 15

Lake Manix, 32, 112, 116
Lake Manly, 9
Lark, horned, 85, 93
Larrea, 159
Lava, 20–22
Lavender, desert, 163
Leafhopper, 48
Lemmon, J. G., 155
Lichens, 152, 153
Lizards, 70–79; Arizona tree uta, 78, 79; banded gecko, 77; Bailey's collared, 77; brown-shouldered, 78; Chuckawalla, 76, 77; Coachella sand, 75; desert scaly, 79; horned, 80; keel-backed, 71; leopard, 74, 75; long-tailed brush, 78; Mearns's uta, 77, 78; night, 79; ocellated sand, 75; whip-tailed, 74; zebra-tailed, 73
Loudermilk, J. D., 153
Lyciums, 162
Lytta, 51

Manix, Lake, 32, 112, 116
Manly, Lake, 9
Mariposa lily, 123
Match weed, 162
Megathymus, 175
Meloids, 51
Mesquite, 174, 175
Messor, 53
Micrarionta, 65
Midges, 48
Millipedes, 62
Minnows, desert, 66, 67
Mistletoe, 177
Mitchell's Caverns, 186
Mites, 61, 62
Mockingbird, 85
Mohave Desert: defined, 3; flower season, 123; weather, 42; winds, 34–37
Mohave River, 10, 11, 12; fish in, 67
Mosaic, desert, 29, 30
Mosquitoes, 49

Mothes, Dr. Kurt, 126
Moths, 57
Mouse: grasshopper, 182; harvest, 103; pocket, 103, 104; white-footed, 102
Mutillids, 55

Nematodes, 65
New York Mountains, 159
Noble, L. F., 13, 19, 186
Nolina, 165, 166

Ocotillo, 166
Old Woman Mountains, 159
Oreohelix, 65
Owens Lake, 8
Owls, 97, 98

Palearctic Desert, 2
Palm, Washingtonia, 180
Palm borer, 180, 181
Palo verde, 176, 177
Parish, S. B., 154
Parkinsonia, 176, 177
Paroselas, 161, 178
Parry, C. C., 154, 155
Pediments, 24
Pergonomyrmex, 54
Petroglyphs, 114
Phainopepla, 94
Phiddipus, 61
Phoebe, Say's, 89
Phoradendron, 183
Phrynosoma, 80
Physa, 65
Pilot Knob, 24
Pinnacles, 9
Piñon, 165, 183, 184
Primrose, evening, 123, 124
Prosopis, 174, 175
Pseudo-scorpion, 59
Puffballs, 151

Quail, Gambel, 85, 88, 89

Rabbit brush, 159
Rabbits, 106, 107
Raccoon, 109
Rainfall, 37, 38, 39
Rats: kangaroo, 100, 101; trade, 103–5
Rattlesnake: Mohave, 82; Panamint, 82; sidewinders, 82, 83; speckled, 82–83; Texas, 82
Raven, 90, 91
Red racer, 83
Ricardo formation, 32
Ring-tailed cat, 109
Roadrunner, 87, 88
Robber flies, 48
Rogers Lake, 9
Rust fungus, 163

Sagebrush, 167
Sahuaro, 181
Salazaria, 161
Salt glands, 80
Saltbush (*Atriplex*), 164
Salton Sea, 15, 16
Salton Sink, 15
San Andreas Rift, 19, 20
San Gorgonio Pass, 36
Sand, work of, 28
Sand storms, 37
Sandpaper bush, 163
Santa Anas, 34, 35
Scale-broom, 162
Scale insects, 47
Scorpions, 58, 59
Screwbean, 175, 176
Scrub oak, 179
Searles Basin and Lake, 9, 10
Selaginella, 155, 156
Schmidt-Nielsen, Dr. Knut, 101
Shrike, 94, 95
Shrubs, 158–73; burroweed, 161; cacti, 167–74; cat's-claw, 176; creosote bush, 159; crucifixion thorn, 166; *Dalea*, 160; desert lavender, 163; *Ephedra*, 160; *Franseria*, 161;

goat-nut, 161, 162; *Hymenoclea*, 162; Indian hemp, 163; *Krameria*, 161; *Lycium*, 162; matchweed, 162; mistletoe, 176, 182, 183; *Nolina*, 165, 166; ocotillo, 166, 167; picklewort, 163; sagebrush, 167; saltbushes, 164; *Salvia dorii*, 159; sandpaper bush, 162; scale-broom, 162; spiny aster, 164; yuccas, 165
Smoke tree, 178
Snakes, 82, 83
Snow, 38, 40
Solpugids, 62, 63
Soda Lake, 12n, 13, 25, 187
Sparrows: bell, 92; black-throated, 91; desert, 91; English, 91; sage, 91; white-crowned, 91
Spiders, 59–61
Sumner, F. B., on animal coloration, 102

Tadpole shrimps, 63
Tamarisk, 179
Termites, 45, 46
Theobaldia, 50
Thomisidae, 61
Thompson, David G., 40
Thrashers, 95, 96
Thrips, 46
Thrush, hermit, 85
Thysanura, 43, 44
Tinajas, 26
Toads, 67–69
Tortoise, 80, 81
Travel hints, 184–87
Trails: Indian, 119; Spanish, 11, 12
Trees, 174–83
Triodia, 157
Tristram, 98, 99
Typha, 157

Urosaurus, 78
Uta: Arizona tree, 78, 79; brown-

shouldered, 78; long-tailed, 78; Mearns's, 77, 78

Varnish, desert, 30
Verdin, 85
Vinegaroon, 62, 63

Warbler: Alaska yellow, 85; Audubon, 91; Lucy, 94
Washingtonia, 165
Wasp, 48, 156
Water: balance of, for birds, 85, 86; for plants, 125, 136; savers and spenders, 43; signs of, 26, 180; supply, 26, 162
Wax scale, 47
Wildcat, 109, 110
Wild flowers of the desert, 122–26; illustration of (127–49):
Acamptopappus sphaerocephalus (golden head), 145
Allium fimbriatum (wild onion), 127
Amsinckia douglasiana, A. tessellata, 143
Anisocoma acaulis, 147
Arabis pulchra, 132
Artemisia spinescens, 145
Aster abatus (Mojave aster), 149
Astragalus casei, A. lentiginosus, 133
Atriplex canescens, A. confertifolia (saltbush), *A. hymenelytra* (desert holly), *A. lentiformis, A. linearis, A. parryi, A. polycarpa*, 130
Audibertia incana pilosa, 142
Beloperone californica (chuperosa), 144
Brickellia atractyloides, B. incana, 146
Calochortus kennedyi (desert mariposa), 127
Canbya candida, 131
Cassia armata (desert cassia), 133

Chaenactis santolinoides, 148; *C. stevioides, C. xantiana*, 149
Chorizanthe brevicornu, 129; *C. corrugata, C. perfoliata, C. rigida, C. spinosa, C. watsoni*, 128
Cleomelia obtusifolia (Mohave stinkweed), 131
Coldenia canescens, C. plicata, 143
Coleogyne famosissima, 133
Condalia canescens, C. parryi (desert jujube), 135
Coreopsis bigelovii, 147
Croton californicus, 137
Ditaxis lanceolata, 137
Dithyrea californica (spectacle pod), 132
Dysodia cooperi, 148
Eremiastrum belloides (desert star), 146
Eriogonum angulosum, E. brevicornis, E. gracillimum, E. inflatum (desert trumpet), *E. indularium*, 129
Eriophyllum wallacei, 157
Eschscholtzia glyptosperma, E. minutiflora (pygmy poppy), 131
Eucnide urens, 136
Euphorbia eriantha, 137
Eurotia lanata (mule fat), 130
Fagonia chilensis laevis, 135
Franseria dumosa (burroweed), 149
Geraea canescens (desert sunflower), 146
Gilia aurea decora, G. brevicula, 139; *G. davyi, G. depressa*, 140; *G. dichotoma* (evening snow), 139; *G. latifolia, G. leptomeria, G. parryae*, 140; *G. setosissima*, 139
Glyptopleura setulosa, 147
Grayia spinosa (hop sage), 130
Gutierrezia californica (match weed), 145

Halliophytum hallii, 137
Heliotropium convolulaceum, 143
Hesperocallis undulata (desert day lily), 127
Hibiscus denudatus (hibiscus), 136
Hoffmannseggia microphylla, 133
Hofmeisteria pluriseta (arrow leaf), 148
Hymenoclea salsola, 145
Hyptis emoryi (desert lavender), 142
Isomeris arborea (bladder pod), 131
Krameria canescens, 134
Larrea tridentata (creosote bush), 135
Lepidium flavum (yellow pepper grass), *L. fremontii* (desert alyssum), 132
Lotus rigidus, 133
Lupinus sparsiflorus arizonicus (lupine), 134
Malacothrix coulteri (snake's head), 147
Malvastrum rotundifolium (five-spot), 136
Mentzelia affinis, 136
Mimulus mohavensis, 144
Mohavea confertiflora, 144
Nama demissum, 140; *N. hispidum coulteri*, 139
Nicolletia occidentalis, 148
Nicotiana trigonophylla (Indian tobacco), 142
Oenothera cardiophylla, O. decorticans condensata, O. deltoides (dune primrose), *O. dentata johnstonii, O. micrantha jonesii*, 138
Orobanche cooperi, 144
Oxytheca luteola, O. perfoliata, O. trilobata, 128

Palafoxia linearis (Spanish needle), 146
Parosela californica, P. parryi, P. schottii, 134. *See also* Smoke tree
Perityle emoryi, 149
Peucephyllum schottii, 146
Phacelia bicolor, P. campanularia, P. crenulata, P. fremontii, 141
Philibertia hirtella (climbing milkweed), 141
Phlox stansburyi, 147
Physalis crassifolia (desert ground cherry), 142
Plantago insularis fastigata, 144
Porophyllum gracile, 148
Psathyrotes annua, 146
Salazaria mexicana, 142
Simmondsia californica (goatnut), 135
Sphaeralcea ambigua (apricot mallow), *S. fendleri*, 136
Stephanomeria runcinata, 149
Stillingia spinulosa, 137
Streptanthus inflatus (squaw cabbage), 132
Tetradymia spinosa, 145
Thamnosma montana (desert rue), 135
Tricardia watsoni, 141
Trixis californica, 145
Viguiera deltoidea parishii, 149
Zygadenus brevibracteatus, 127
Winds: "evening blow," 36; Santa Ana, 34, 35; whirlwinds, 37
Woodpecker, Texas, 88
Wren, cactus, 92; rock, 85, 95

Xantusia, 79

Yucca borer, 182
Yuccas, 165, 181, 182
Yumans, 115, 118, 120

Zygadene, 122